CUPS AND SAUCERS

PAPER-PIECED KITCHEN DESIGNS

MAAIKE BAKKER

Martingale
& COMPANY

Bothell, Washington

CREDITS

President ⌒ Nancy J. Martin
CEO ⌒ Daniel J. Martin
Publisher ⌒ Jane Hamada
Editorial Director ⌒ Mary V. Green
Editorial Project Manager ⌒ Tina Cook
Design and Production Manager ⌒ Stan Green
Technical Editor ⌒ Ursula Reikes
Copy Editor ⌒ Ellen Balstad
Illustrator ⌒ Laurel Strand
Photographer ⌒ Brent Kane
Cover and Text Designer ⌒ Rohani Design

Cups and Saucers: Paper-Pieced Kitchen Designs
© 2000 by Maaike Bakker

Martingale & Company
PO Box 118
Bothell, WA 98041-0118 USA
www.patchwork.com

05 04 03 02 01 00   6 5 4 3 2 1

Mission Statement
We are dedicated to providing quality products
and service by working together to inspire creativity
and to enrich the lives we touch.

Library of Congress Cataloging-in-Publication Data

Bakker, Maaike.
   Cups and saucers / Maaike Bakker.
      p. cm.
      ISBN 1-56477-333-7
      1. Patchwork—Patterns. 2. Patchwork quilt. I. Title.

TT835 .B263 2000
746.46'041—dc21
                                          00-063798

DEDICATION

To Hilly Oosterloo. Without her help and support, this book would not be a reality.

ACKNOWLEDGMENTS

You never write a book on your own. Thanks to:
Joke Griffioen, Rosa Hultink, Françoise Maarse, Janneke Neuteboom,
Bartina Noorman, Hanneke van Nus, Hilly Oosterloo, Lydie Roeland, Erika
Schoenmakers, Marijke Schortinghuis, and Saskia de Vries for their warm support and
their help in making the quilts; Françoise Maarse, Saskia de Vries, and Henny Werring
for reading the manuscript; Tom Griffioen for solving all my computer problems;
Wim Dooren for taking my photograph; and Theo Claas, my husband,
for doing the word processing.

CONTENTS

INTRODUCTION

Paper piecing is an excellent technique for quickly and accurately making blocks for patchwork quilts. The process is a simple one: cut fabrics in a particular size and sew them to a paper foundation in numerical order. The technique allows you to create block designs that you would have a difficult time making with more traditional piecing methods. Even blocks with very small pieces and sharp points are quick and easy to make with paper piecing.

Take a close look at the quilts in this book. I'm sure you'll agree that the idea of making some of the blocks with tiny little templates is not very appealing. But with paper piecing there is no need for templates. You don't even have to cut the fabric accurately. You simply have to cut the fabric pieces big enough to fit the appropriate space, and sew them in numerical order.

Paper piecing is suitable for beginning quiltmakers as well as more experienced ones. This book contains many wonderful block designs. Beginners will enjoy making the easy block and quilt designs, while the more complicated designs will be a challenge for even the most experienced quiltmaker. You can use the blocks to make the quilts as shown in the book, or use the blocks to create your own quilt designs.

I have shared my enthusiasm for paper piecing with a great number of students, and they all love the technique as well as my quilt designs. It was their enthusiasm that inspired me to write books about paper piecing. I hope you, too, will become enthusiastic about paper piecing and my quilts.

Maaike Bakker

PAPER PIECING

Supplies

Supplies for paper piecing are simple and few.

- Tracing or lightweight paper
- Sharp pencil
- Ruler
- Scissors
- Pins
- Sewing machine
- Rotary cutter and mat
- Access to a copy machine (optional)

Reproducing the Block Designs

The first step in paper piecing is to trace or photocopy the block designs presented in the book. You will need one copy for each block you plan to use in your quilt. If you don't have access to a copy machine, trace the design and numbers onto tracing paper with a ruler and pencil. If you can make copies on a copy machine, be sure to make all copies for each project on the same copy machine; different copy machines may produce copies that are slightly different in size.

Creating a Reverse Image

The block designs printed in this book represent the wrong side of the blocks. In a symmetrical design the finished block will be the same as the printed block design. In an asymmetrical design the finished block will be the reverse of the printed block design. For example, notice the handle on the following Teapot block design. It is on the left-hand side of the printed block design. This means that it will be on the right-hand side of the finished block. If you want the handle on the left-hand side of the finished block, you will need to reverse the printed block design.

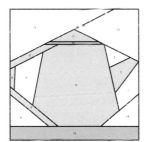
Block design in book

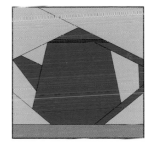
Finished block—
handle on right-hand side

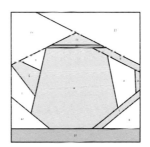
Reverse of the printed
block design in book

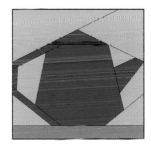
Finished block—
handle on left-hand side

You can reverse a block design by tracing it onto lightweight paper. Then redraw the lines on the reverse side of the paper, which will be the side you sew on. Use a light table or tape the design to a window to help you see the lines through the paper. Be sure to write *reverse* on the paper so that you know which side to sew on. Photocopy the reverse image instead of tracing it multiple times if you need to make more than one reverse image of the block.

Enlarging or Reducing the Block Designs

The blocks used in the quilts are 6" x 6" finished, with a few additional blocks in smaller sizes. Several 9" x 9" and 4½" x 4½" blocks are included for use in place mat projects. You can use a copy machine to enlarge or reduce the blocks if you want to use different block sizes for the projects in this book.

Original Finished Size	Desired Finished Size	Enlargement or Reduction Percentage
6"	9"	150 percent enlargement
6"	4½"	75 percent reduction
4½"	9"	200 percent enlargement
4½"	6"	133 percent enlargement
3"	6"	200 percent enlargement

Cutting Fabric Pieces

The most important thing to remember about cutting the fabric pieces for paper piecing is that they must be cut large enough to cover the designated area plus at least ¼" seam allowances all the way around. If you are new to paper piecing, I have developed a method to help you figure out how to cut the fabric pieces so that they will fit the designated areas, including seam allowances. For this method, make two copies of a block design. Use one as the paper foundation for paper piecing. Cut the other copy into pieces and use the pieces as patterns for cutting the fabric. Pin these pattern pieces to the wrong side of the fabric and cut around them, adding a generous ¼" seam allowance all around. You can use a rotary cutter or scissors. This seam allowance does not have to be perfect; you can just eyeball it. Keep the pattern pieces pinned to the fabric until you are ready to use them.

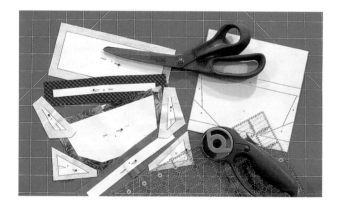

When cutting fabrics for paper piecing, you do not need to pay attention to the straight of grain because the paper provides the stability that prevents the fabric pieces from stretching as they are sewn. However, if you use plaids, stripes, or other directional fabrics, the final result will be more attractive if you do pay attention to the straight of grain.

Piecing the Blocks

1. Pin fabric piece #1 right side up to the unmarked side of the paper foundation, covering area #1. If you reversed the block design, pin your fabric to the side of the paper foundation that is not marked *reverse*. Make sure the fabric covers the area completely and extends at least ¼" on all sides. Hold the paper and fabric up to a light source, with the marked side of the paper toward you, to help you position the fabric.

2. With right sides together, pin fabric piece #2 on top of piece #1. Make sure piece #2 extends at least ¼" beyond the seam lines. You can check the placement of piece #2 by pinning the fabric at the seam between pieces #1 and #2 and opening up piece #2; it should cover area #2 completely, plus seam allowances.

3. Place the paper, marked side up, under the presser foot and sew on the seam line between areas #1 and #2. Use a very small stitch to make removing the paper easier. Backstitch at the beginning and end of the seam.

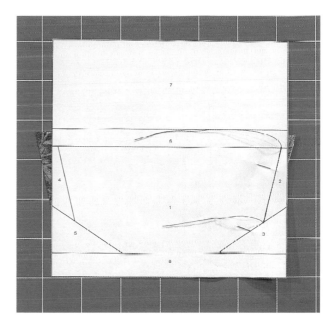

4. Trim away any excess fabric so that the seam allowance is about ¼" wide. Open up piece #2 and finger-press or use an iron to press the seam. Add fabric piece #3 to area #3 with the same method described in step 2, and sew on the line between areas #2 and #3. Backstitch at the beginning and end of the seam. Trim the seam allowance to ¼", open piece #3, and press the seam.

5. Continue adding pieces in numerical order until the block design is complete.

6. Press the finished block. Place the block on the cutting mat with the paper side up. Trim the edges of the block, leaving ¼"-wide seam allowances beyond the outside lines. Do not remove the paper yet.

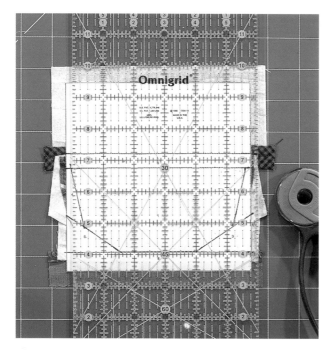

USING A RULER WITH PAPER PIECING

If you want to use plaids or stripes, or if you have to piece very odd-shaped fabric pieces, you can use a ruler to trim excess fabric from one piece before positioning the next piece.

Pin fabric piece #1, right side up, to the unmarked side of the paper foundation, covering area #1. Fold the paper on the line between areas #1 and #2. Lay the work on a cutting mat with the fabric side down. You will now see a portion of fabric piece #1 extending beyond the folded paper. Cut this excess fabric to ¼" from the edge of the paper to make an exact ¼"-wide seam allowance. Open up the folded paper. With right sides facing, pin fabric piece #2 to piece #1 along the just-trimmed raw edges of piece #1. Sew on the line between areas #1 and #2. Open up piece #2 and press. Repeat for all pieces.

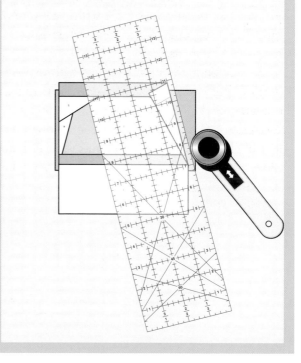

PLANNING A QUILT

If you want to use the blocks to make your own quilt design, it is a good idea to do some planning first. Decide on the measurements of the quilt and make an accurate drawing of your design. Color the drawing so that you can see how your color choices will look. Of course you can change your plans during the work, but an accurate plan can be a great help.

Choosing Colors

Select colors you like. Also realize that the prospective surroundings and the function of the quilt are important when you choose colors. However, two of the most important things to remember when selecting colors are have courage and take risks. Do not try to make the colors match too well. Otherwise, your quilt may end up dull and monotonous. A quilt becomes a great quilt when something unexpected happens.

Be sure that there is sufficient contrast: either contrast between light and dark, or contrast between complementary colors. Take a good look at the fabrics by squinting or looking through a red piece of glass or plastic. Good contrasts will remain visible when viewed this way. Looking at a colored sketch in this way is also a good opportunity to analyze contrast.

Notice the effects of using warm colors (yellows, oranges, and reds) and cool colors (greens, blues, and violets). Warm colors seem nearer than they are, which is why they are called advancing colors. Cool colors appear to be farther away and are called receding colors. Use this knowledge when choosing colors for the background or foreground. Light and dark hues also have similar effects: light colors seem nearer than they are and dark colors appear to be farther away.

Washing the Fabrics

It is wise to wash all fabrics before using them. Some fabrics will shrink, and you will also see which fabrics are not colorfast. Wash the fabrics at the same temperature you will use when washing the finished project.

ASSEMBLING THE QUILT TOP

Assembling the Center

After piecing the blocks and trimming them with ¼"-wide seam allowances, arrange them in a pleasing manner. Keep playing with them until you are satisfied with the results. Add plain blocks and sashing strips to the arrangement if your quilt has them.

To sew the blocks into rows, place the right sides of the blocks together and align the raw edges. Sew from edge to edge along the outside line of the paper-piecing design. Stitch with an exact ¼"-wide seam allowance. Press the seam allowances in opposite directions from row to row. This will keep the intersection seams neat and flat.

Join the rows to make the center of the quilt top. If your quilt has sashing strips and cornerstones, sew them into rows and join them with the rows of blocks.

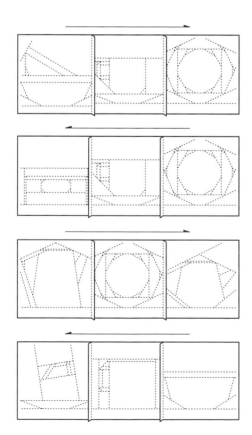

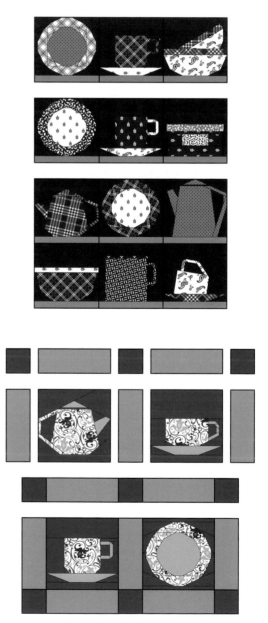

Mitering Corners

Mitered corners are used for the construction of the top of the cupboards in "Kitchen Cupboard," "Delft Ceramics," and "Narrow Cupboard." The following steps describe how to sew mitered corners.

1. On the wrong side of the quilt, mark the ¼" seam intersections on the top corners.

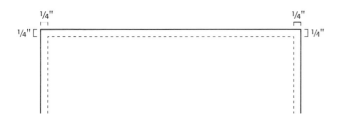

2. With right sides together, pin the strip for the top of the cupboard to the quilt. The strip is longer than the top of the quilt and will extend beyond the edges a few inches. Turn the quilt over and stitch from corner to corner as marked on the wrong side of the quilt.

3. With right sides together, pin the strips for the wall to the sides of the quilt. The strips will extend beyond the top edge a few inches. On the wrong side of the quilt, stitch from the corner mark at the top of the quilt to the bottom edge of the quilt. On the remaining side, stitch from the bottom edge to the top corner mark.

4. For one corner, fold the quilt top diagonally with wrong sides together so that the strips for the cupboard top and wall are aligned, with right sides together.

5. Use a ruler to draw a line at a 45° angle from the end of the stitch line to the outside edge.

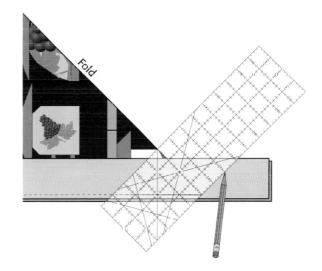

6. Stitch on the drawn line. Trim excess fabric to ¼" from the seam. Press the seam allowance open.

7. Repeat steps 4–6 for the other corner.

Adding Borders

All the quilts in this book have straight-cut corners. Cut the border strips to match the length and width measurements of the quilt. The width of the border strips is indicated in the project directions. Mark the centers of the sides of the quilt top and the centers of the border strips. With right sides together, pin the border strips to the quilt top, matching the ends and centers. Stitch the borders to the quilt top with ¼"-wide seam allowances. Press the seams toward the border strips. Repeat for the top and bottom borders. Repeat with additional borders as required.

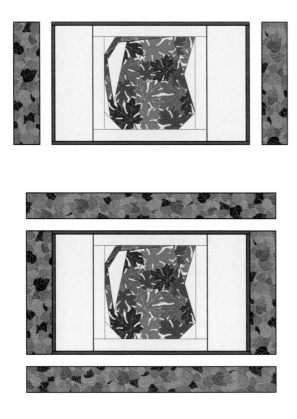

For a border with corner squares, first sew the side borders to the sides of the quilt. Then sew a corner block to each end of the top and bottom strips. Join these to the quilt top.

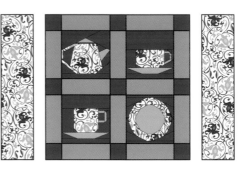

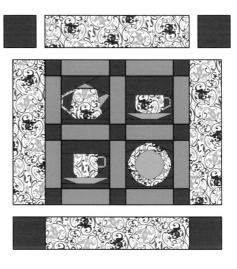

Removing the Paper

After assembling the quilt top, you can remove the paper. Rub the block between your hands until the paper creases and begins to tear. Carefully remove the paper. For small pieces of paper, you can use a pair of tweezers. Do not worry about removing the last tiny scraps of paper. Press the quilt top after the paper is removed.

FINISHING THE QUILT

Marking the Quilt Design

Mark the quilt top before basting the layers together unless you intend to outline-quilt or stitch in the ditch, in which case it is not necessary to mark the quilting lines.

Layering and Basting the Quilt

Cut the backing fabric and batting 3" or 4" larger than the quilt top all around. In this book the fabric requirements are based on 42"-wide fabric. For quilts larger than 40", the backing must be pieced. The batting must also be pieced on large quilts.

To piece the batting, stitch as shown below. Make sure that the pieces of batting butt against each other and do not lie on top of each other. Whipstitch the pieces together.

Once your backing is ready, lay it right side down on a clean and smooth surface such as a floor or a table. Be sure that the backing lies smooth and wrinkle-free. Secure the backing with masking tape to the floor or table. Lay the batting on the backing, smoothing out any wrinkles. Then lay the pressed quilt top on the batting.

Smooth the top with your hands from the center to the edges. Pin the layers together with lots of straight pins. Start in the center and work toward the edges. Remove the masking tape and move the quilt to a table if it is not already on one. For hand quilting, baste the layers together with needle and thread, making a grid of basting stitches about 4" apart. For machine quilting, baste with safety pins. Place the safety pins 6" to 8" apart, away from the area you intend to quilt. Always baste from the center of the quilt toward the edges. Once you have basted the layers together, remove the straight pins.

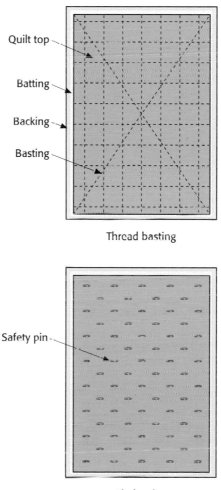

Thread basting

Pin basting

Quilting

Quilting can be used to emphasize your pieced design. A quilting line about 1/16" outside and all around the design will make the design come forward a little. All the designs in this book were outline-quilted 1/16" away from the edges of the design.

To make a design recede, quilt about 1/16" inside the edges of the design.

Continuous quilting designs such as diagonal lines and stipple quilting are suitable for quilting large areas. They help connect the pieced designs and unify the quilt. You can also use quilting to add related designs, such as the hearts around "Welcome" or the cups and saucers in the open spaces on "Delft Ceramics."

Hand Quilting

If you prefer hand quilting, keep in mind that paper-pieced blocks may be a bit bulky. Very few of the quilts have large areas of a single layer of fabric for hand quilting. The plain blocks and borders are areas that are more suitable for hand quilting.

After marking the quilt (if applicable) and basting the layers together, place the quilt in a hoop. Use thimbles on both hands to protect your fingers.

To begin, do not make a knot in your thread; instead, take two stitches on top of each other. Quilt with a small, even running stitch. Insert the needle vertically through the three layers. Cant the needle with your left hand under the quilt. Push the needle upward with your right middle finger. Repeat this several times until you have a number of stitches on your needle, and then pull the thread through. End your stitching by taking two stitches on top of each other, and then run the thread through the batting before snipping the ends.

Machine Quilting

Layer and baste the quilt as described in "Layering and Basting the Quilt" on page 13. For straight-line quilting, attach a walking foot to your sewing machine if you have one. A walking foot is very helpful because it allows you to guide the layers of the quilt through the sewing machine evenly. Always work from the center outward. Secure the beginning and ending stitches by changing the stitch length to zero and taking about five stitches in place. Do not sew too fast. If you need to turn a corner, stop with the needle in the down position before raising the presser foot.

For free-motion quilting, attach a darning foot and lower or cover the feed dogs. The stitch length is determined by the speed at which you run the machine and feed the fabric under the foot. Try to move your hands slowly and the foot pedal at a fairly fast, even speed. Do not turn the fabric under the needle. Instead, guide the fabric under the needle. Begin and end your stitching by taking a few stitches in place.

Stipple quilting is a good way to fill a background and is easy to do. Shapes are formed with a continuous motion. The stitching lines should not cross or look too uniform. It's a good idea to practice before you start your quilt.

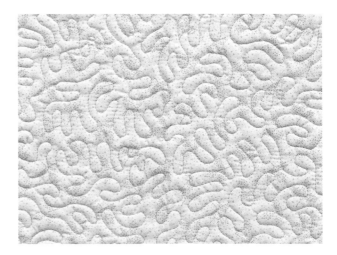

When you are comfortable with stipple quilting you can try other free-motion quilting designs. Draw designs directly on the quilt top with a water-soluble marking pen and stitch on the drawn lines. Or, if you prefer not to draw directly on the quilt, you can make a paper pattern of a quilting design. To make a paper pattern, trace one of the designs on pages 58 and 77–79, or draw your own design on lightweight paper. Pin the pattern in place on the quilt top and free-motion stitch the design. Make sufficient copies for the quilt. Don't forget to secure the beginning and the end of your stitching. Remove the paper carefully. Use tweezers to remove tiny scraps.

Adding a Sleeve

To hang a wall quilt, you must have a hanging sleeve to slip a rod through. Use the same fabric as the backing so that it will blend in.

1. Cut a strip of fabric as long as the width of the quilt and about 5" wide for a small quilt, or 7" wide for a large one. Hem both ends of the strip.

2. Fold the strip lengthwise, wrong sides together. Baste the strip to the back side of the quilt, matching the raw edges at the top of the quilt, before you attach the binding.

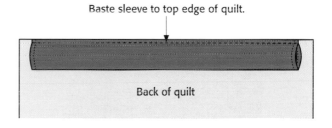

Baste sleeve to top edge of quilt.

Back of quilt

3. Add the binding to the quilt as stated below. Blindstitch the folded edge of the sleeve to the back of the quilt after the binding has been added.

Blindstitch folded edge in place.

Binding

All the quilts in this book were bound with double-fold bias binding that finishes to ½". The place mats were bound with double-fold bias binding that finishes to ¼".

To cut double-fold bias binding strips:

1. Fold the fabric for the binding as shown. Pay careful attention to the location of the lettered corners.

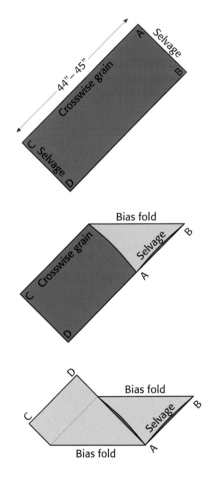

2. For the quilts, cut strips 3" wide. Cut perpendicular to the folds as shown. You will need enough 3"-wide strips to go around the perimeter of the quilt plus 10" for seams. For place mats, cut strips 2¼" wide.

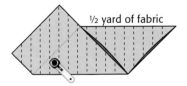

½ yard of fabric

To attach the binding:

1. Trim the batting and backing even with the edges of the quilt top. I like to make rounded corners on my quilts so that I can sew the binding to the quilt without having to miter the corners. To make slightly rounded corners, place the edge of a teacup on each corner and draw around the curve from one side of the quilt to the other. Cut on the drawn line. For corners that are more rounded, try a saucer or dinner plate.

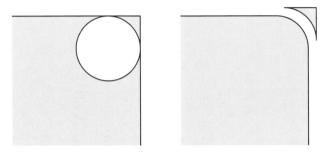

2. Join binding strips, right sides together, with a ¼" seam allowance to make one long piece of binding. Press the seams open.

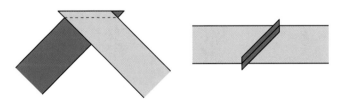

3. Fold the binding in half, wrong sides together; press.

4. Align the raw edges of the binding with the raw edges of the quilt. Leaving the first 10" of binding unsewn, stitch the binding in place with a ½"-wide seam allowance. (Use a ¼"-wide seam allowance on place mats.) Before you get to a corner, pin the binding around the curve before you sew. Gently ease the binding around the curve. Do not stretch the binding as you pin it in position. If the binding is stretched, the corner will not lie flat.

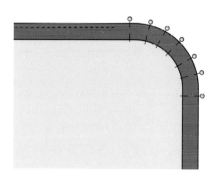

5. Continue around the edges of the quilt, gently easing the binding around the remaining corners.

6. When you are within 10" of the starting point, remove the quilt from the sewing machine and lay the unsewn section on a flat surface. Fold the unsewn binding ends back on themselves so that they just meet in the middle over the unsewn area of the quilt top. Finger-press or pin both binding ends to mark this junction.

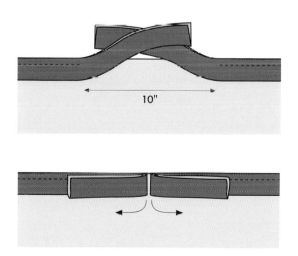

10"

7. Unfold both ends of the binding. With right sides facing, match the centers of the pressed Xs. Sew across the intersection as when sewing the binding strips together. Trim the excess fabric and press the seam open. Finish stitching the binding to the quilt edge.

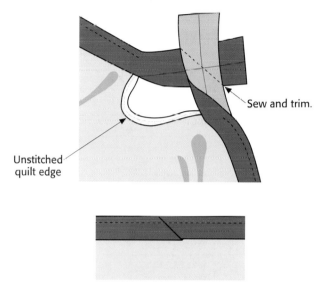

Sew and trim.

Unstitched quilt edge

8. Fold the binding over the raw edges to the back of the quilt. Blindstitch in place, with the folded edge covering the row of machine stitching.

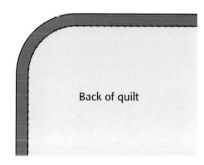

Back of quilt

HIGH TEA

High Tea by Maaike Bakker and Hilly Oosterloo, 1999, Diever, The Netherlands.
Make a portrait of your crockery for your kitchen or dining room.

Finished Quilt Size: 23" x 23"

Alternative

Blue Dishes by Maaike Bakker and Hilly Oosterloo, 1999, Diever, The Netherlands, 23" x 23".

Materials for "High Tea"

42"-wide fabric

¼ yd. green solid for sashing
⅜ yd. dark green solid for block backgrounds,
    cornerstones, and corner squares
⅝ yd. floral print for blocks and outer border
¼ yd. pale green solid for blocks
¾ yd. for backing
26" x 26" piece of batting
½ yd. for bias binding

Cutting

Cut the following pieces before making blocks.
All measurements include ¼"-wide seam allowances.

From the green solid, cut:
    12 strips, each 2" x 6½" (A)

From the dark green solid, cut:
    9 squares, each 2" x 2" (B)
    4 squares, each 3½" x 3½" (D)

From the floral print, cut:
    4 strips, each 3½" x 17" (C)

Block Assembly

Trace or photocopy four 6" block designs of your choice. Block patterns begin on page 48. Reverse the block designs if desired (see page 5). Referring to the directions on pages 7–8, paper piece the blocks. Trim the blocks, leaving ¼"-wide seam allowances beyond the outside lines of the block pattern.

Quilt Top Assembly

1. Arrange the blocks as shown. Sew 2 paper-pieced blocks and 3 sashing strips (A) together. Sew 3 cornerstones (B) and 2 sashing strips (A) together. Repeat for the remaining blocks, sashing strips, and cornerstones. Join the rows of blocks and rows of sashing.

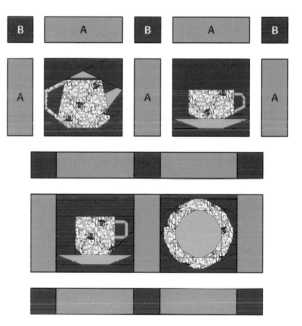

2. Sew the 3½" x 17" outer border strips (C) to the sides of the quilt. Press the seams toward the border strips. Sew a corner square (D) to each end of the remaining border strips (C) and attach these to the top and bottom edges; press.

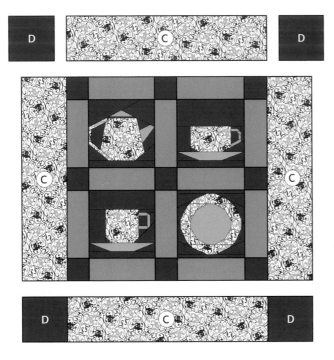

Quilt Finishing

1. Layer the quilt top with batting and backing; baste.
2. Outline-quilt the block designs. Quilt ¹⁄₁₆" inside the sashing strips. The border of "High Tea" is quilted with a strawberry design. The border of "Blue Dishes" is quilted with an apple design. See page 58 for the quilt patterns.
3. Attach a hanging sleeve.
4. Bind the edges of the quilt.

WELCOME

Welcome by Maaike Bakker and Hilly Oosterloo, 1999, Diever, The Netherlands.
This quilt will welcome every visitor if it is hanging near the entrance of your house.
It tells your visitors that you are an enthusiastic quiltmaker.

Finished Quilt Size: 42½" x 32½"

Materials

42"-wide fabric

1 yd. light blue print for block backgrounds, inner border, and quilt background pieces

¼ yd. dark blue solid for shelf and middle border

⅝ yd. multicolored plaid for outer border

½ yd. total of assorted red and blue fabrics for blocks

1⅜ yds. for backing

47" x 38" piece of batting

½ yd. for bias binding

Cutting

Cut the following pieces before making blocks.
All measurements include ¼"-wide seam allowances.

From the light blue print, cut:
1 rectangle, 3½" x 4" (A)
3 rectangles, each 1½" x 4" (B)
1 strip, 4" x 6½" (C)
6 rectangles, each 1" x 3½" (D)
1 rectangle, 2½" x 3½" (E)
1 strip, 5" x 26½" (F)
2 strips, each 2" x 17½" (G)
2 strips, each 3½" x 33½" (H)

From the dark blue solid, cut:
2 strips, each 1" x 23½" (I)
2 strips, each 1" x 34½" (J)

From the multicolored plaid, cut:
2 strips, each 4½" x 24½" (K)
3 strips, each 4½" x 42" (L)

Block Assembly

Trace or photocopy the blocks listed in the chart above right. Reverse the block designs if desired (see page 5) except for the letter blocks. Block patterns begin on page 48. Referring to the directions on pages 7–8, paper piece the blocks. Trim the blocks, leaving ¼"-wide seam allowances beyond the outside lines of the block pattern.

Blocks (Size)	Number to Make	Page Number
Cookie Tin (6")	1	67
Hanging Mug (3½")	4	53
Milk Jug (6")	1	54
Plate (6")	2	61
Towel (4" x 11")	1	76
Two Bowls (6")	1	60
W (3")	1	57
E (3")	2	55
L (3")	1	56
C (3")	1	55
O (3")	1	57
M (3")	1	56

Quilt Top Assembly

1. Arrange and sew the blocks and background pieces together as shown. Sew the 2" x 17½" inner border strips (G) to the sides of the quilt. Press the seams toward the border strips. Sew the remaining 3½" x 33½" inner border strips (H) to the top and bottom edges; press.

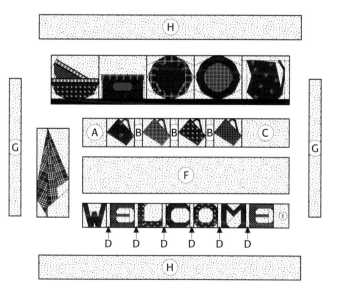

2. Sew the 1" x 23½" middle border strips (I) to the sides of the quilt. Press the seams toward the middle border strips. Sew the remaining 1" x 34½" middle border strips (J) to the top and bottom edges; press.

3. Sew the 4½" x 24½" outer border strips (K) to the sides of the quilt. Press the seams toward the outer border strips. Sew the three remaining 4½" x 42" outer border strips together to make one long strip. From the long strip, cut 2 pieces, each 4½" x 42½" (L). Sew these to the top and bottom edges; press.

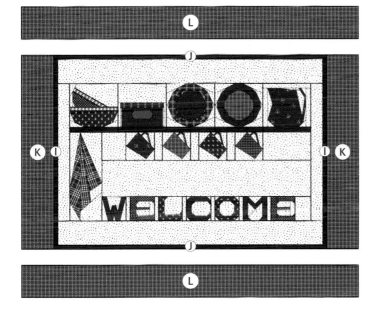

Quilt Finishing

1. Layer the quilt top with batting and backing; baste.
2. Outline-quilt the dishes, the towel, the letters, and the inner border. Fill the background with stipple quilting. The border is quilted with a heart design.
3. Attach a hanging sleeve.
4. Bind the edges of the quilt.

Creative Option

Arrange the letters vertically to make a "welcome" wall hanging for your front door.

TABLE RUNNER

Table Runner *by Maaike Bakker and Hilly Oosterloo, 1999, Diever,*
The Netherlands. This table runner, made of warm-colored fabrics,
will look beautiful on a light or dark wooden table.

Finished Quilt Size: 24½" x 66½"

Materials

42"-wide fabric

1½ yds. orange print for block backgrounds, outer
     border, and background squares
¾ yd. plaid for blocks and inner border*
1 yd. total of assorted check, plaid, or striped
     fabrics for blocks
⅛ yd. green solid for blocks
¼ yd. dark brown solid for shelves
28" x 70" piece of batting
1¾ yds. for backing
½ yd. for bias binding

** Yardage requirements are for cutting inner borders on the
bias. If you prefer to cut straight-grain strips, you will need
only ½ yard of fabric for the blocks and inner border.*

Cutting

Cut the following pieces before making blocks.
All measurements include ¼"-wide seam allowances.

From the orange print, cut:
     8 squares, 6½" x 6½" (A)
     5 strips, 2½" x 42" (for D and E)

**From the plaid, cut bias strips as follows if you
want the plaid to be on the bias.****
     Cut enough 1½"-wide bias strips so that you
          can sew them together and from this long
          strip cut 2 strips, each 1½" x 60½" (B),
          and 2 strips, each 1½" x 20½" (C), for
          inner borders.

*** If you prefer to cut straight-grain strips, cut 4 strips, each
1½" x 42". Sew the strips together to make one long strip.
From this strip, cut inner border strips in sizes indicated
above.*

Block Assembly

Trace or photocopy the 6" blocks listed in the chart
below. Reverse the block designs if desired (see page
5). Block patterns begin on page 48. Referring to
directions on pages 7–8, paper piece the blocks.
Trim the blocks, leaving ¼"-wide seam allowances
beyond the outside lines of the block pattern. Use
the dark brown solid for the piece at the bottom of
each block and on the side of the Plate blocks used
in the 4 corners. This will create the shelf around
the table runner.

Blocks	Number to Make	Page Number
Bowl	1	59
Cup and Saucer 1	3	55
Cup and Saucer 2	2	56
Cup and Saucer 3	1	57
Milk Jug	1	54
Mug	3	58
Pile of Plates	2	64
Plate in Corner	4	65
Plate	2	61
Teapot	1	48
Two Bowls	2	60

Quilt Top Assembly

1. Arrange and sew the blocks and background squares (A) together as shown. Join the rows.

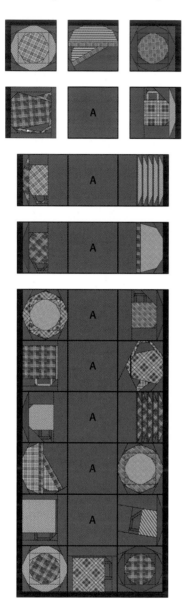

2. Sew the 1½" x 60½" inner border strips (B) to the long sides of the table runner. Press the seams toward the border strips. Sew the 1½" x 20½" inner border strips (C) to the short sides of the table runner; press.

3. Sew the five 2½" x 42" orange-print outer border strips together to make one long strip. From the long strip, cut 2 strips, each 62½" long (D) and 2 strips, each 24½" long (E). Sew

the D strips to the long sides of the quilt and the E strips to the short sides. Press the seams toward the outer borders.

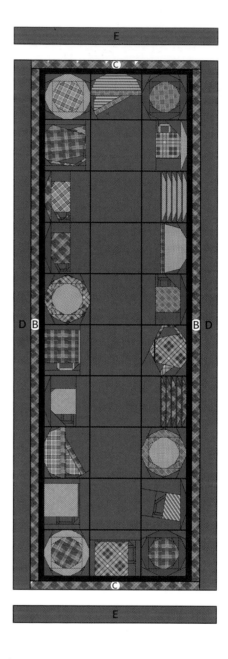

Quilt Finishing

1. Layer the quilt top with batting and backing; baste.

2. Outline-quilt the dishes. The center is quilted with the leaf design found on page 78. Outline-quilt the borders about 1/16" away from the seam.

3. Bind the edges of the quilt.

KITCHEN CUPBOARD

Kitchen Cupboard by Maaike Bakker, Joke Griffioen, Rosa Hultink, Janneke Neuteboom,
Bartina Noorman, Hanneke van Nus, Hilly Oosterloo, Lydie Roeland, Erika Schoenmakers,
Marijke Schortinghuis, and Saskia de Vries, 2000, Diever, The Netherlands.
Eleven women made the blocks for this quilt, all using the same background fabric.
Paper piecing is very appropriate for making a quilt with a group of people, because the
technique ensures that there will be no differences in the sizes of the blocks.

Finished Quilt Size: 45½" x 58"

Materials

42"-wide fabric

½ yd. brown solid for shelves and cupboard

1 yd. burgundy print for block backgrounds and
    top of cupboard

⅝ yd. ecru solid for block backgrounds and wall

¼ yd. red solid for inner border

¾ yd. red-and-white plaid for outer border

¼ yd. each of several red and blue prints and
    plaids for blocks

Scraps of gold print and white solid for Jam Jar
    block

49" x 61" piece of batting

3 yds. for backing

½ yd. for bias binding

Cutting

Cut the following pieces before making blocks.
All measurements include ¼"-wide seam allowances.

From the brown solid, cut:
    2 strips, each 1½" x 36½" (A)
    1 strip, 1½" x 32½" (B)
    1 strip, 2½" x 36½" (D)
    1 strip, 1" x 24½" (G)

From the burgundy print, cut:
    1 strip, 1" x 36½" (F)

From the ecru solid, cut:
    1 strip, 3½" x 22½" (C)
    3 strips, 2½" x 42" (for E)
    1 strip, 6" x 24½" (H)

From the red solid, cut:
    5 strips, each 1" x 42" (for I and J)

From the red-and-white plaid, cut:
    5 strips, each 4½" x 42" (for K and L)

Block Assembly

Trace or photocopy the block designs listed in the chart above right, which are all 6" except for Cupboard Leg 2 block, which is 3" x 5". Reverse the block designs if desired (see page 5). Block patterns begin on page 48. Referring to the directions on pages 7–8, paper piece the blocks. Use the burgundy print for the background in all blocks except as noted. Use the brown solid for the bottom piece in all blocks to create the shelves in the cupboard. Trim the blocks, leaving ¼"-wide seam allowances beyond the outside lines of the block pattern.

Blocks	Number to Make	Page Number
Cookie Tin	2 (1 with ecru background)	67
Bowl	2	59
Coffeepot	2	49
Cup and Saucer 1	5	55
Cup and Saucer 2	3	56
Cup and Saucer 3	2	57
Cupboard Leg 2	2 (both with ecru background)	66
Jam Jar	1	74
Milk Jug	2 (1 with ecru background)	54
Mug	3	58
Pile of Plates	2	64
Plate	3	61
Teapot	2	48
Two Bowls	3	60

Quilt Top Assembly

1. Arrange and sew the blocks together in horizontal rows as shown on facing page. Join the rows.

2. Sew the 1½" x 36½" brown strips (A) to the sides of the quilt. Press the seams toward the border strips. Sew the 1½" x 32½" strip (B) to the bottom; press.

3. Sew a Cupboard Leg 2 block to each side of the 3½" x 22½" ecru strip (C). Sew this to the bottom of the quilt. Press the seam toward the brown strip.

4. Sew the 2½" x 36½" brown strip (D) to the top of the quilt, referring to "Mitering Corners" on page 11. Sew three 2½" x 42" ecru strips together to make one long strip. From the long strip, cut 2 pieces, each 2½" x 42½" (E). Sew these to the sides of the quilt, mitering the

corners. Press the seams toward the brown strips.

5. Sew the 1" x 36½" burgundy strip (F) to the top of the quilt. Press the seams toward the burgundy strip.

6. Sew the 1" x 24½" brown strip (G) to the 6" x 24½" ecru strip (H). Press the seam toward the brown strip. To this unit, add the two 6" blocks with ecru backgrounds to the left side, and sew the strip to the top of the quilt.

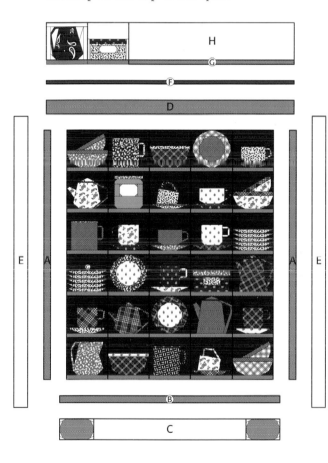

7. Sew the five 1" x 42" red-solid inner border strips together to make one long strip. From the long strip, cut 2 strips, each 1" x 49" (I), and 2 strips, each 1" x 37½" (J). Sew the longer strips (I) to the sides of the quilt. Press the seams toward the inner border strips. Sew the remaining inner border strips (J) to the top and bottom edges; press.

8. Sew the five 4½" x 42" red-and-white plaid outer border strips together to make one long strip. From the long strip, cut 2 strips, each 4½" x 50" (K), and 2 strips, each 4½" x 45½" (L). Sew the K strips to the sides of the quilt. Press the seams toward the outer border strips. Sew the L strips to the top and bottom edges; press.

Quilt Finishing

1. Layer the quilt with batting and backing; baste.
2. Outline-quilt the blocks, the cupboard, and the inner border. The wall is quilted with the flower pattern on page 78. The outer border is quilted with a border design made with the help of a quilting stencil.
3. Attach a hanging sleeve.
4. Bind the edges of the quilt.

SUMMER PLACE MATS

Summer Place Mats *by Maaike Bakker, 2000, Diever, The Netherlands.*
It is nice setting the table with these place mats on a sunny summer morning.

Finished Size: 18½" x 14"

Materials for 4 Place Mats

42"-wide fabric

¼ yd. red solid for inner border
½ yd. plaid for outer border
¾ yd. burgundy print for block backgrounds
¾ yd. total assorted fabrics for blocks
4 pieces, each 16" x 21", of batting
⅞ yd. for backing
½ yd. for bias binding

Cutting for 4 Place Mats

Cut the following pieces before making blocks.
All measurements include ¼"-wide seam allowances.

From the red solid for inner border, cut:
  8 strips, each ¾" x 9½" (A)
  8 strips, each ¾" x 14½" (B)

From the plaid for outer border, cut:
  8 strips, each 2½" x 10" (C)
  8 strips, each 2½" x 18½" (D)

Block Assembly

Trace or photocopy one 9" block design and two 4½" block designs of your choice for each place mat. Reverse the block designs if desired (see page 5). Block patterns begin on page 48. Referring to the directions on pages 7–8, paper piece the blocks. Trim the blocks, leaving ¼"-wide seam allowances beyond the outside lines of the block pattern.

PLACE MAT 1		
Blocks (Size)	**Number to Make**	**Page Number**
Strawberry (4½")	2	69
Two Bowls (9")	1	68–69

PLACE MAT 2		
Blocks (Size)	**Number to Make**	**Page Number**
Cereal Bowl (4½")	1	53
Jam Jar (4½")	1	63
Milk Jug (9")	1	52–53

PLACE MAT 3		
Blocks (Size)	**Number to Make**	**Page Number**
Cup and Saucer 1 (4½")	1	51
Cup and Saucer 2 (4½")	1	51
Teapot (9")	1	50–51

PLACE MAT 4		
Blocks (Size)	**Number to Make**	**Page Number**
Apple (4½")	1	63
Cup and Saucer 1 (4½")	1	51
Plate (9")	1	62–63

Place Mat Assembly

Follow the steps below to make each place mat.

1. Arrange and sew the blocks together, referring to the color photo on facing page.
2. Sew the ¾" x 9½" inner border strips (A) to the sides of the place mat. Press the seams toward the border strips. Sew the remaining ¾" x 14½" inner border strips (B) to the top and bottom edges; press.

3. Sew the 2½" x 10" outer border strips (C) to the sides of the place mat. Press the seams toward the outer border strips. Sew the remaining 2½" x 18½" (D) outer border strips to the top and bottom edges; press.

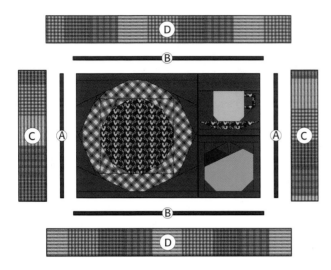

Place Mat Finishing

1. Layer the place mats with batting and backing; baste.
2. Outline-quilt the block designs and the inner border.
3. Bind the edges of the place mats.

Creative Option: Potholders

Make two 9" blocks of your choice. Layer the blocks with a piece of cotton batting and a piece of backing, all 10" x 10". Quilt the blocks. Bind the potholders with bias binding, making a loop in one corner.

DELFT CERAMICS

Delft Ceramics by Maaike Bakker, Joke Griffioen, Rosa Hultink, Janneke Neuteboom, Bartina Noorman, Hanneke van Nus, Hilly Oosterloo, Lydie Roeland, Erika Schoenmakers, Marijke Schortinghuis, and Saskia de Vries, 2000, Diever, The Netherlands. The Delft crockery in this cupboard was made by eleven women. Delft Blue crockery has been made in the Netherlands for many centuries.

Finished Quilt Size: 59½" x 63½"

Materials

42"-wide fabric

⅞ yd. brown print for shelves and cupboard

1¾ yds. dark blue solid for background, cupboard top, and inner border

1¾ yds. blue-and-white striped fabric for wall (stripe runs along lengthwise grain)

1¾ yds. blue-and-white floral for outer border

¼ yd. each of several blue prints and plaids for blocks

Scraps of gold print and white solid for Jam Jar blocks

63" x 68" piece of batting

4 yds. for backing

¾ yd. for bias binding

Cutting

Cut the following pieces before making blocks.
All measurements include ¼"-wide seam allowances.

From the brown print, cut:

> 2 strips, each 1⅛" x 6½", for bottom shelf of plain blocks
>
> 3 strips, each 2" x 42" (for A)*
>
> 1 strip, 2" x 39½"(B)
>
> 2 strips, each 3½" x 42" (for D)
>
> 2 strips, each 1½" x 42" (for G)

*If your fabric happens to be 42½" wide, then you need only to cut 2 strips for A. Otherwise, you'll need to cut 3 strips and join them as directed in step 2 under "Quilt Top Assembly."

From the dark blue solid, cut:

> 2 rectangles, each 5⅞" x 6½", for plain blocks in cupboard
>
> 2 strips, each 1½" x 42" (for F)
>
> 6 strips, each 1" x 42" (for J and K)

From the blue-and-white striped fabric, cut the following strips from the crosswise and lengthwise grains as indicated. You must cut strips from both fabric grains to keep the stripes running vertically in the quilt.

> 1 strip, 3½" x 27½", from the crosswise grain (C)

> 2 strips, each 3" x 42", from the crosswise grain (for H)
>
> 2 strips, each 3½" x 50", from the lengthwise grain (E)
>
> 2 strips, each 3" x 54½", from the lengthwise grain (I)

From the lengthwise grain of the blue-and-white floral, cut:

> 2 strips, each 4½" x 55½" (L)
>
> 2 strips, each 4½" x 59½" (M)

Block Assembly

Trace or photocopy the block designs listed in the chart below, which are all 6" except for Cupboard Leg 3 block, which is 3" x 6". Reverse the block designs if desired (see page 5). Block patterns begin on page 48. Referring to the directions on pages 7–8, paper piece the blocks. Use the dark blue solid for the background in all blocks except as noted. Use the brown print for the bottom piece in all blocks to create the shelves in the cupboard. Trim the blocks, leaving ¼"-wide seam allowances beyond the outside lines of the block pattern.

Blocks	Number to Make	Page Number
Cookie Tin	3	67
Bowl	4	59
Coffeepot	2	49
Cup and Saucer 1	5	55
Cup and Saucer 2	4	56
Cup and Saucer 3	1	57
Cupboard Leg 3	2 (with blue-and-white striped background)	67
Jam Jar	4	74
Milk Jug	2	54
Mug	3	58
Pile of Plates	4	64
Plate	4	61
Teapot	1	48
Two Bowls	3	60

Quilt Top Assembly

1. Sew a 1⅛" x 6½" brown strip to the bottom of each 5⅞" x 6½" dark blue square to make the 2 plain blocks in the cupboard. Arrange and sew the paper-pieced blocks and the 2 plain blocks together as shown. Join the rows.

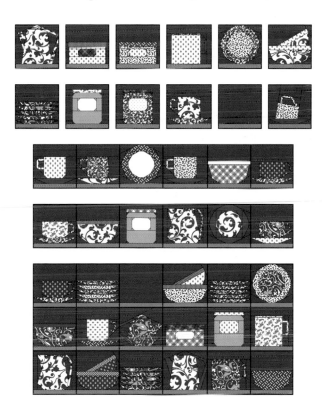

2. If your brown fabric was not 42½" wide, you will need to sew the three 2" x 42" brown strips together to make one long strip. From the long strip, cut 2 strips, each 2" x 42½" (A) and sew these to the sides of the quilt. Press the seams toward the border strips. Sew the 2" x 39½" brown strip (B) to the bottom; press.

3. Sew a Cupboard Leg 3 block to each side of the 3½" x 27½" blue-and-white striped fabric strip (C). Sew this to the bottom of the quilt. Press the seam toward the blue-and-white strip.

4. Sew the two 3½" x 42" brown strips together to make one long strip. From the long strip, cut a 3½" x 45½" strip (D). Following the directions for "Mitered Corners" on page 11, sew the D strip to the top of the quilt and the 3½" x 50" blue-and-white striped fabric strips (E) to the sides. Press the seams toward the D and E strips.

5. Sew the two 1½" x 42" dark blue strips together to make one long strip. From the long strip, cut a 1½" x 45½" strip (F), and sew this to the top of the quilt. Sew the two 1½" x 42" brown strips together to make one long strip. From the long strip, cut a 1½" x 45½" strip (G), and sew this to the top of the quilt. Sew the two 3" x 42" blue-and-white striped fabric strips together to make one long strip. From the long strip, cut a 3" x 45½" strip (H), and sew this to the top of the quilt. Press all of the seams toward the top of the cupboard.

6. Sew the 3" x 54½" blue-and-white striped fabric strips (I) to the sides of the quilt. Press the seams toward the blue-and-white strips.

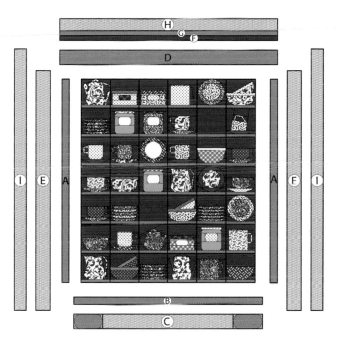

7. Sew the six 1" x 42" dark blue strips together to make one long strip. From the long strip, cut 2 strips, each 1" x 54½" (J), and 2 strips, each 1" x 51½" (K), for the inner border. Sew the J strips to the sides of the quilt and the K strips to the top and bottom edges. Press the seams toward the inner border strips.

8. Sew the 4½" x 55½" outer border strips (L) to the sides of the quilt. Press the seams toward the outer border strips. Sew the remaining 4½" x 59½" (M) outer border strips to the top and bottom edges; press.

Quilt Finishing

1. Layer the quilt with batting and backing; baste.
2. Outline-quilt the dishes and the cupboard. The wall is quilted with the flower pattern on page 77. The outer border is quilted with a border design made with the help of a quilting stencil.
3. Attach a hanging sleeve.
4. Bind the edges of the quilt.

NARROW CUPBOARD

Narrow Cupboard by Maaike Bakker and Hilly Oosterloo, 1999, Diever, The Netherlands.
*This long and narrow quilt does not need much space. You can even hang
it on a door if the walls in your kitchen are already filled.*

Finished Quilt Size: 29½" x 45"

Materials

42"-wide fabric

⅜ yd. gold print for cupboard
½ yd. burgundy print for block backgrounds, cupboard top, and inner border
½ yd. green print for wall
½ yd. dark green print for outer border
⅛ yd. each of several purple and green prints for blocks
Small scraps of white and yellow fabrics for candles, cookie tin label, and flames in blocks
33" x 48" piece of batting
1⅜ yds. backing fabric
½ yd. for bias binding

Cutting

Cut the following pieces before making blocks.
All measurements include ¼"-wide seam allowances.

From the gold print, cut:
   2 strips, each 1½" x 30½" (A)
   1 strip, 1" x 14½" (B)
   1 strip, 2½" x 18½" (D)
   1 strip, 1" x 18½" (G)

From the burgundy print, cut:
   1 strip, 1" x 18½" (F)
   2 strips, each 1" x 38" (J)
   2 strips, each 1" x 23½" (K)

From the green print, cut:
   1 strip, 2½" x 9½" (C)
   2 strips, each 2½" x 35" (E)
   2 strips, each 2½" x 36" (H)
   1 strip, 2½" x 22½" (I)

From the dark green print, cut:
   2 strips, each 3½" x 39" (L)
   2 strips, each 3½" x 29½" (M)

Block Assembly

Trace or photocopy the block designs listed in the chart above right, which are all 6" except for Cupboard Leg 1 block, which is 2" x 2½", and the Candle blocks, which are 3" x 6". Reverse the block designs if desired (see page 5). Block patterns begin on page 48. Referring to the directions on pages 7–8, paper piece the blocks. Use the burgundy print for the background in all blocks except as noted. Use the gold print for the bottom piece in all blocks to create the shelves in the cupboard. Trim the blocks, leaving ¼"-wide seam allowances beyond the outside lines of the block pattern.

Blocks (Size)	Number to Make	Page Number
Cookie Tin	1	67
Candle	2	64
Cup and Saucer 1	1	55
Cupboard Leg 1	2 (with green print background)	65
Milk Jug	1	54
Pile of Plates	1	64
Plate	2	61
Soup Tureen	1	66
Teapot	1	48
Two Bowls	1	60

Quilt Top Assembly

1.   Arrange and sew the blocks together as shown. Join the rows.

2. Sew the 1½" x 30½" gold strips (A) to the sides of the quilt. Press the seams toward the border strips. Sew the 1" x 14½" gold strip (B) to the bottom; press.

3. Sew a Cupboard Leg 1 block to each side of the 2½" x 9½" green print strip (C). Sew this strip to the bottom of the quilt. Press the seam toward the green strip.

4. Following the directions on page 11 for "Mitered Corners," sew the 2½" x 18½" gold strip (D) to the top of the quilt, and the 2½" x 35" green print strips (E) to the sides. Press the seams toward the top and sides of the quilt.

5. Sew the 1" x 18½" burgundy strip (F) and the 1" x 18½" gold strip (G) to the top of the quilt. Press the seams toward the top of the quilt.

6. Sew the 2½" x 36" green print strips (H) to the sides of the quilt. Press the seams toward the green strips. Sew the 2½" x 22½" green print strip (I) to the top of the quilt; press.

7. Sew the 1" x 38" burgundy strips (J) to the sides of the quilt. Press the seams toward the burgundy strips. Sew the 1" x 23½" burgundy strips (K) to the top and bottom edges; press.

8. Sew the 3½" x 39" dark green strips (L) to the sides of the quilt. Press the seams toward the dark green strips. Sew the remaining 3½" x 29½" dark green strips (M) to the top and bottom edges; press.

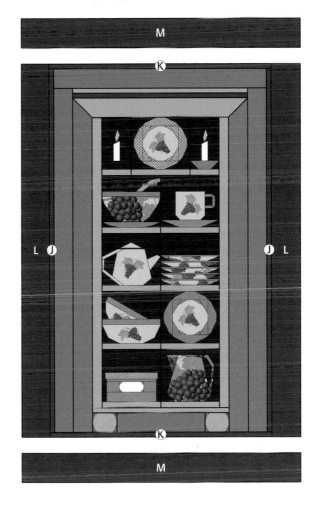

Quilt Finishing

1. Layer the quilt with batting and backing; baste.
2. Outline-quilt the objects, the cupboard, and the inner border. The wall is quilted with stipple quilting. The outer border is quilted with a simple border design found on page 79.
3. Attach a hanging sleeve.
4. Bind the edges of the quilt.

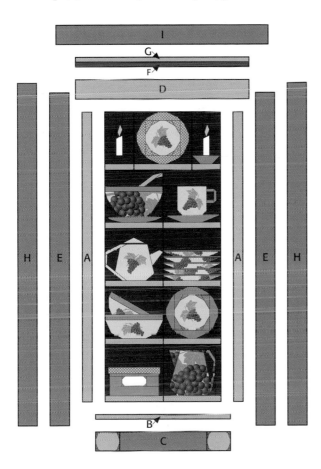

HARVEST

Harvest by Maaike Bakker and Hilly Oosterloo, 1999, Diever, The Netherlands.
To make this basket surrounded with vegetables and fruit, select fabrics that fit the
theme of the quilt. They will make your quilt look even better.

Finished Quilt Size: 27½" x 32"

Materials

42"-wide fabric

½ yd. gold print for Basket block background

¼ yd. dark green for Corn and Pumpkin block backgrounds

⅛ yd. green print #1 for Mushroom block background

⅛ yd. green print #2 for Strawberry block background

⅜ yd. brown print for the Basket block

¼ yd. brown print for Apple block background

½ yd. total assorted fabrics for fruit, vegetables, and basket bow in blocks

31" x 35" piece of batting

⅞ yd. for backing

⅜ yd. for bias binding

Cutting

Cut the following pieces before making blocks.
All measurements include ¼"-wide seam allowances.

From the gold print, cut:
2 strips, each 2" x 15½" (A)
2 strips, each 2" x 18½" (B)

From dark green print, cut:
2 strips, each 1¼" x 18½" (C)

From green print #1, cut:
2 strips, each 1¼" x 18½" (D)

From green print #2, cut:
2 strips, each 1¼" x 27½" (E)

Block Assembly

Trace or photocopy the block designs listed in the chart below. Reverse the block designs if desired (see page 5). Block patterns begin on page 48. Referring to the directions on pages 7–8, paper piece the blocks. Trim the blocks, leaving ¼"-wide seam allowances beyond the outside lines of the block pattern.

Blocks (Size)	Number to Make	Page Number
Apple (4½")	6	63
Basket (15")	1	70–73
Corn (3" x 9")	2	75
Mushroom (3")	6	74
Pumpkin (4½" x 9")	3	75
Strawberry (3")	9	69

Quilt Top Assembly

1. Sew the 2" x 15½" gold strips (A) to the sides of the Basket block. Press the seams toward the gold strips. Sew the 2" x 18½" gold strips (B) to the top and bottom edges of the Basket block; press.

2. Sew the 2 Corn blocks together in a vertical row. Sew the 1¼" x 18½" dark green strips (C) to the sides of the Corn blocks. Press the seams toward the strips.

3. Sew the 6 Mushroom blocks together in a vertical row. Sew the 1¼" x 18½" green print #1 strips (D) to the sides of the Mushroom blocks. Press the seams toward the strips.

4. Sew the 9 Strawberry blocks together in a horizontal row. Sew the 1¼" x 27½" green print #2 strips (E) to the top and bottom of the Strawberry blocks. Press the seams toward the strips.

5. Sew the 3 Pumpkin blocks together in a horizontal row.

6. Sew 6 Apple blocks together in a horizontal row.

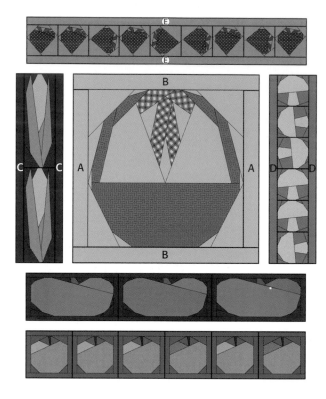

7. Join the row of Corn blocks and the row of Mushroom blocks to the sides of the Basket block. Sew the row of Strawberry blocks to the top of the quilt. Sew the row of Pumpkin blocks to the bottom, and then add the row of Apple blocks to the bottom of the Pumpkin block row. Press the seams toward the rows as you sew them to the quilt top.

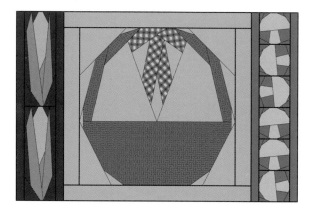

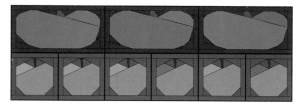

Quilt Finishing

1. Layer the quilt with batting and backing; baste.
2. Outline-quilt the block designs. Quilt a flower design in the corners of the Basket block with the pattern on page 77.
3. Attach a hanging sleeve.
4. Bind the edges of the quilt.

AUTUMN PLACE MATS

Autumn Place Mats *by Maaike Bakker and Hilly Oosterloo, 1999, Diever, The Netherlands.*
These place mats are practical as well as beautiful. Make place mats to match your crockery.

Finished Place Mat Size: 19" x 14"

Materials for 4 Place Mats

42"-wide fabric

¾ yd. yellow print for block backgrounds
¼ yd. dark green print for inner borders
¼ yd. each of 4 autumn prints for outer borders
¼ yd. each of 4 autumn prints for blocks
4 pieces, each 16" x 21", of batting
⅞ yd. for backing
½ yd. for bias binding

Cutting for 4 Place Mats

Cut the following pieces before making blocks.
All measurements include ¼"-wide seam allowances.

From the yellow print, cut:
8 strips, each 3" x 9½" (A)

From the dark green print, cut:
8 strips, each ¾" x 9½" (B)
8 strips, each ¾" x 15" (C)

From each of the 4 autumn prints for outer borders, cut:
2 strips, each 2½" x 10" (D) (8 total)
2 strips, each 2½" x 19" (E) (8 total)

Block Assembly

Trace or photocopy the 9" block designs listed in the chart below. Reverse the block designs if desired (see page 5). Block patterns begin on page 48. Referring to the directions on pages 7–8, paper piece the blocks. Trim the blocks, leaving ¼"-wide seam allowances beyond the outside lines of the block pattern.

Blocks (Size)	Number to Make	Page Number
Milk Jug	1	52–53
Plate	1	62–63
Teapot	1	50–51
Two Bowls	1	68–69

Place Mat Assembly

Follow the steps below to make each place mat.

1. Sew two 3" x 9½" yellow strips (A) to the sides of a block.
2. Sew two ¾" x 9½" inner border strips (B) to the sides of the place mat. Press the seams toward the inner border strips. Sew two ¾" x 15" inner border strips (C) to the top and bottom edges; press.
3. Sew two 2½" x 10" outer border strips (D) to the sides of the place mat. Press the seams toward the outer border strips. Sew two 2½" x 19" outer border strips (E) to the top and bottom edges; press. Make sure to use D and E strips that have been cut from the same fabric.

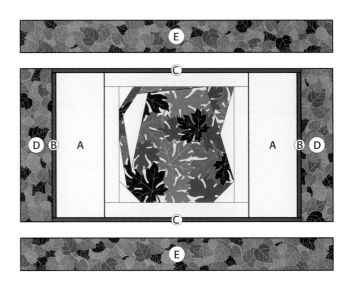

Place Mat Finishing

1. Layer the place mats with batting and backing; baste.
2. Outline-quilt the objects and the inner border. Quilt a flower design in the background with the design found on page 77.
3. Bind the edges of the place mats.

BREAKFAST

Breakfast by Maaike Bakker, 2000, Diever, The Netherlands.
Make this delightful little quilt for your kitchen or breakfast area.

Finished Quilt Size: 15½" x 33½"

Materials

42"-wide fabric

⅛ yd. yellow print 1 for inner border
⅛ yd. blue solid for middle border
¼ yd. blue-and-yellow print for outer border and Jam
    Jar block
¼ yd. yellow print 2 for block backgrounds
½ yd. total assorted blue prints and plaids for
    blocks
Scraps of green and orange fabrics for Apple block
Scrap of white solid for Jam Jar block
19" x 37" piece of batting
⅝ yd. for backing
⅜ yd. for bias binding

Cutting

Cut the following pieces before making blocks.
All measurements include ¼"-wide seam allowances.

From the yellow print #1, cut:
    2 strips, each 1" x 27½" (A)
    2 strips, each 1" x 10½" (B)

From the blue solid, cut:
    2 strips, each 1" x 28½" (C)
    2 strips, each 1" x 11½" (D)

**From the blue-and-yellow print for outer border,
cut:**
    2 strips, each 2½" x 29½" (E)
    2 strips, each 2½" x 15½" (F)

Block Assembly

Trace or photocopy the block designs listed in the chart below. Reverse the block designs if desired (see page 5). Block patterns begin on page 48. Referring to the directions on pages 7–8, paper piece the blocks. Trim the blocks, leaving ¼"-wide seam allowances beyond the outside lines of the block pattern.

Blocks (Size)	Number to Make	Page Number
Apple (4½")	1	63
Cereal Bowl (4½")	1	53
Cup and Saucer 1 (4½")	1	51
Jam Jar (4½")	1	63
Plate (9")	1	62–63
Teapot (9")	1	50–51

Quilt Top Assembly

1. Arrange and sew the blocks together as shown.

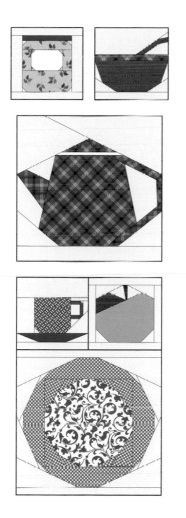

2. Sew the 1" x 27½" inner border strips (A) to the sides of the quilt. Press the seams toward the border strips. Sew the 1" x 10½" inner border strips (B) to the top and bottom; press.
3. Sew the 1" x 28½" middle border strips (C) to the sides of the quilt. Press the seams toward the middle border strips. Sew the 1" x 11½" middle border strips (D) to the top and bottom edges; press.

4. Sew the 2½" x 29½" outer border strips (E) to the sides of the quilt. Press the seams toward the outer border strips. Sew the 2½" x 15½" outer border strips (F) to the top and bottom edges; press.

Quilt Finishing

1. Layer the quilt with batting and backing; baste.
2. Outline-quilt the objects and the inner border. Stipple-quilt the background. The border is quilted with the border design found on page 79.
3. Attach a hanging sleeve.
4. Bind the edges of the quilt.

BLOCK PATTERNS AND QUILTING DESIGNS

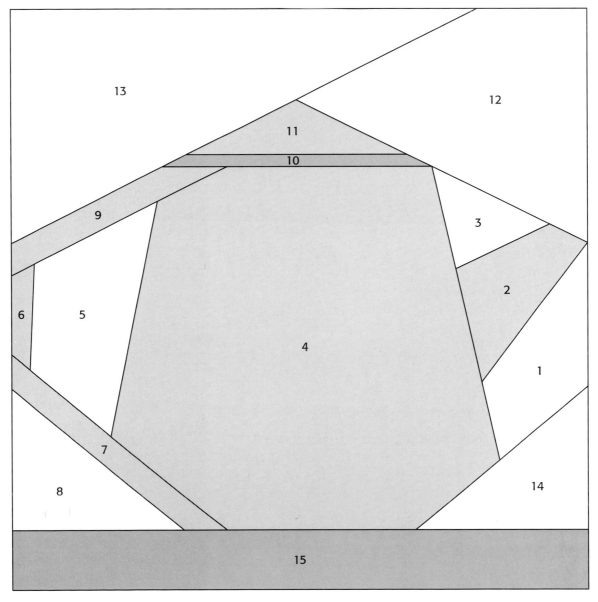

Teapot
6"

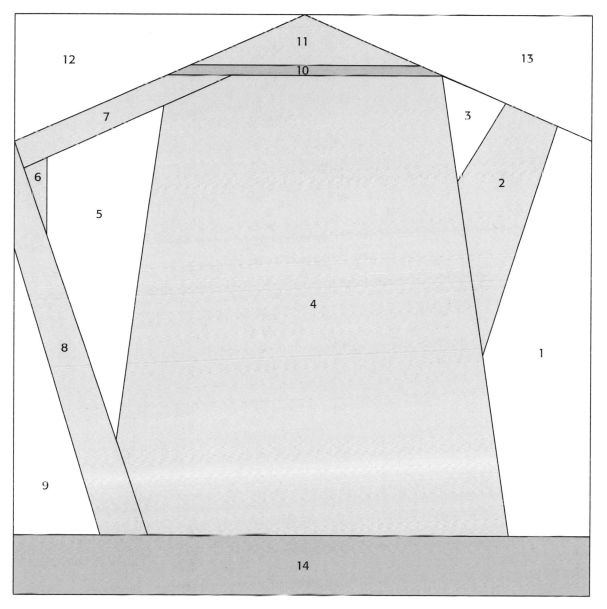

Coffeepot
6"

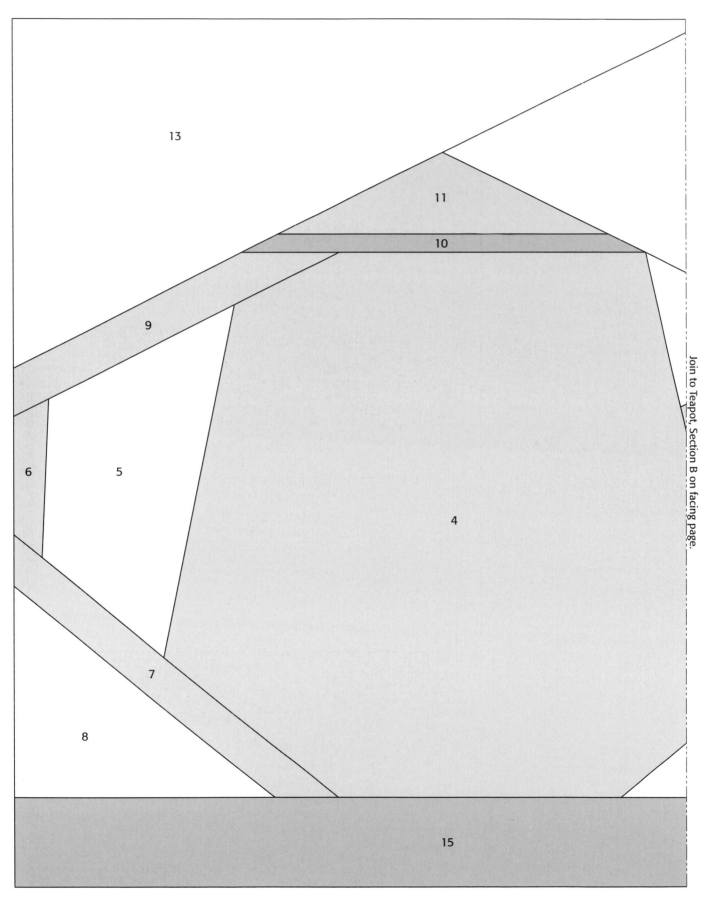

Join to Teapot, Section B on facing page.

Teapot, Section A
9"

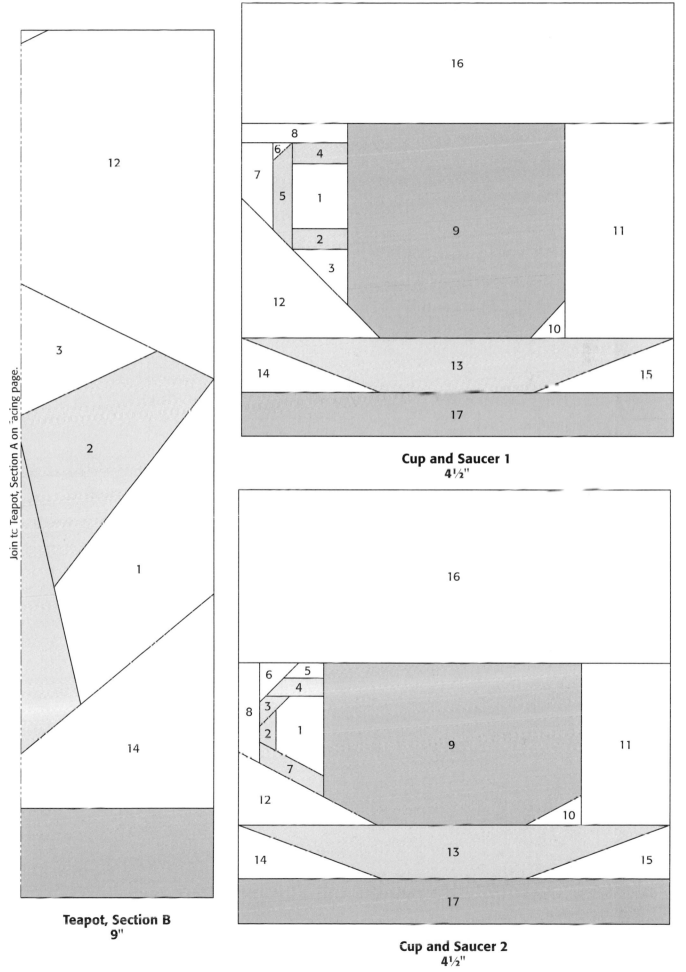

Cup and Saucer 1
4½"

Teapot, Section B
9"

Cup and Saucer 2
4½"

Join to Teapot, Section A on facing page.

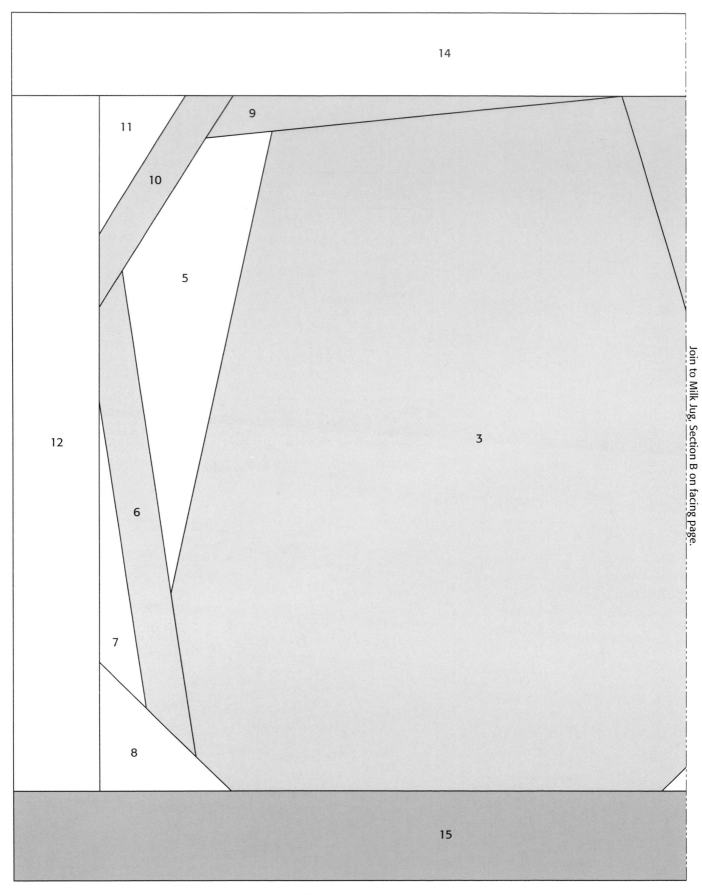

Milk Jug, Section A
9"

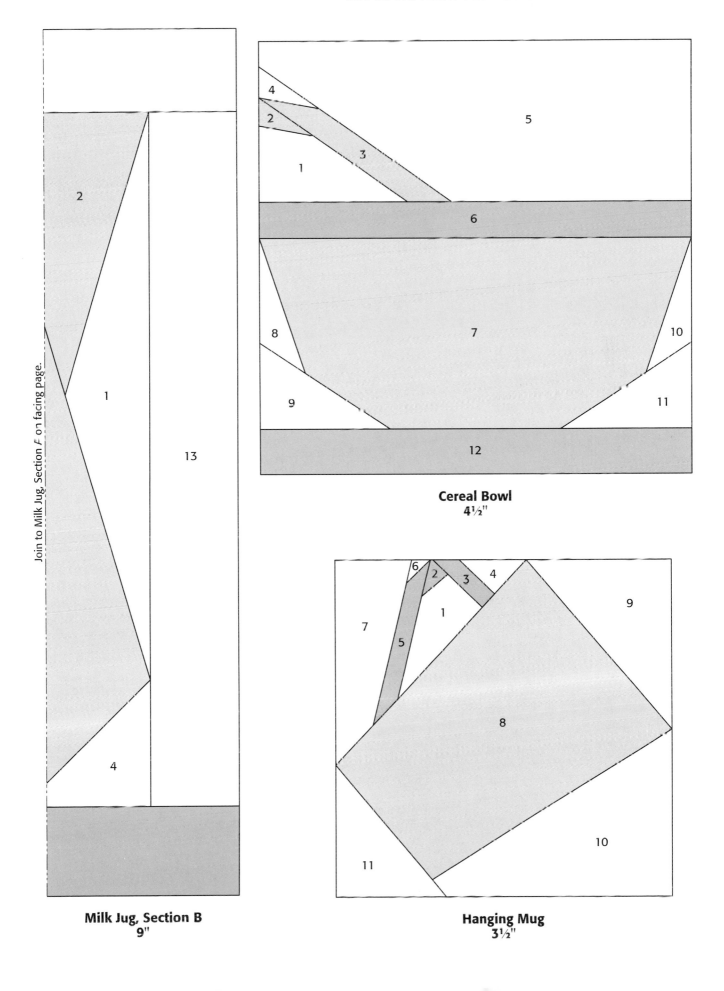

Join to Milk Jug, Section F on facing page.

Cereal Bowl
4½"

Milk Jug, Section B
9"

Hanging Mug
3½"

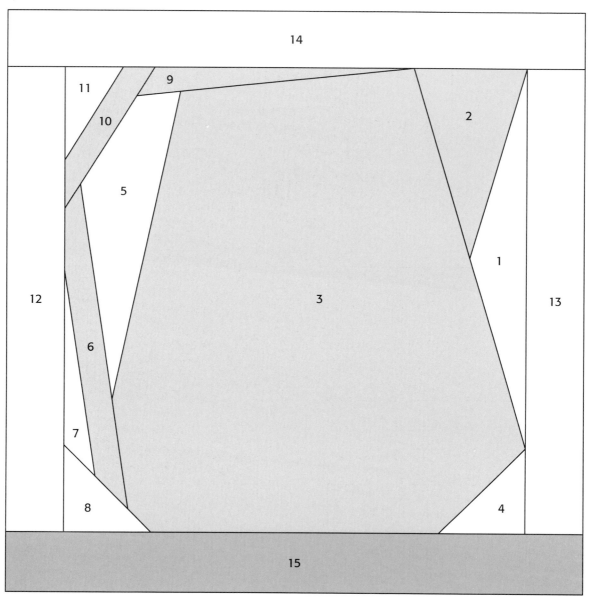

Milk Jug
6"

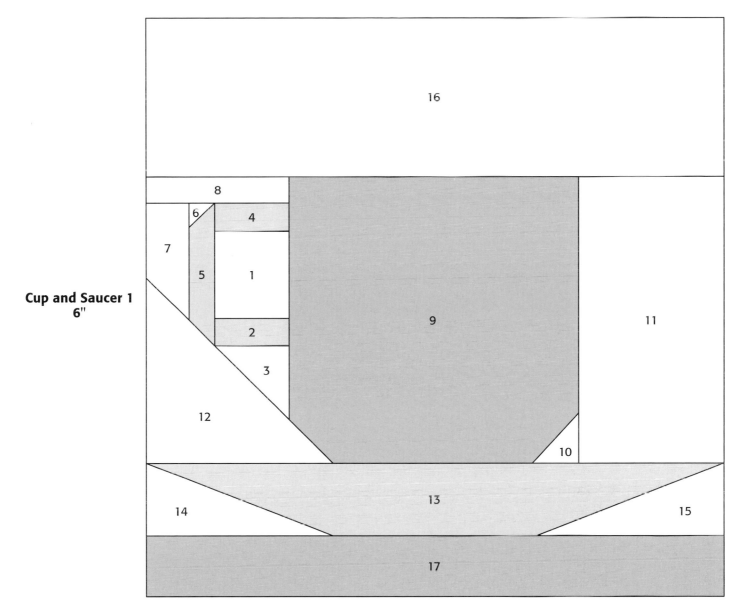

Cup and Saucer 1
6"

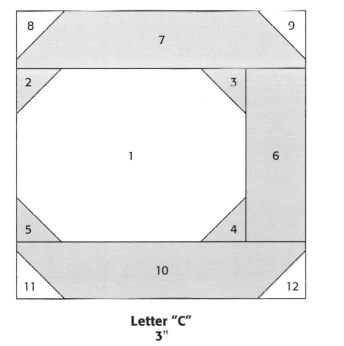

Letter "C"
3"

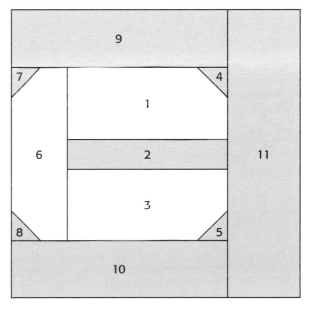

Letter "E"
3"

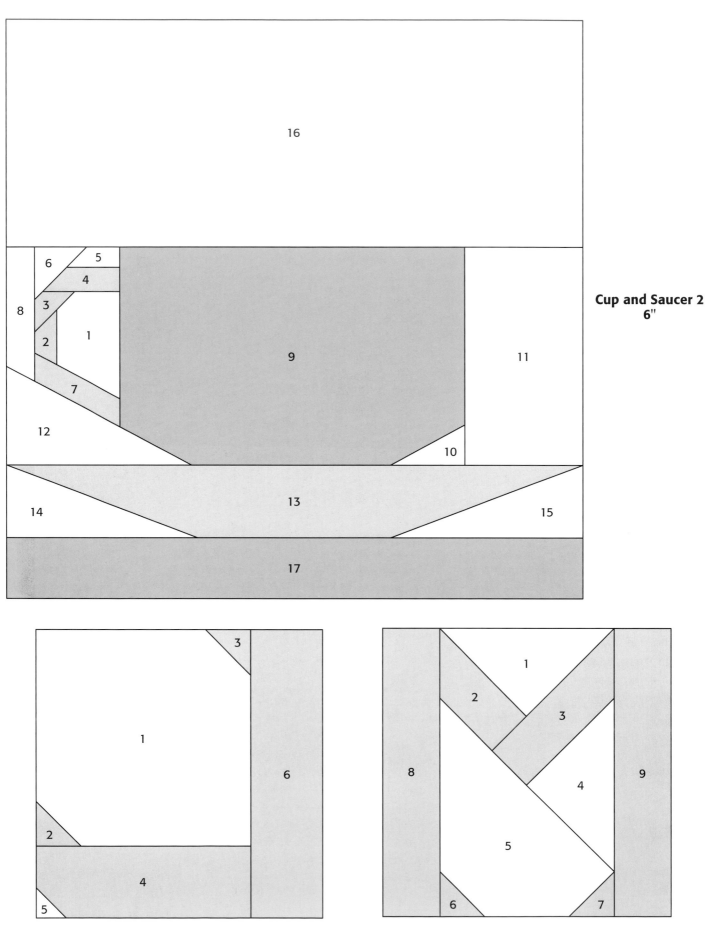

Cup and Saucer 2
6"

Letter "L"
3"

Letter "M"
3"

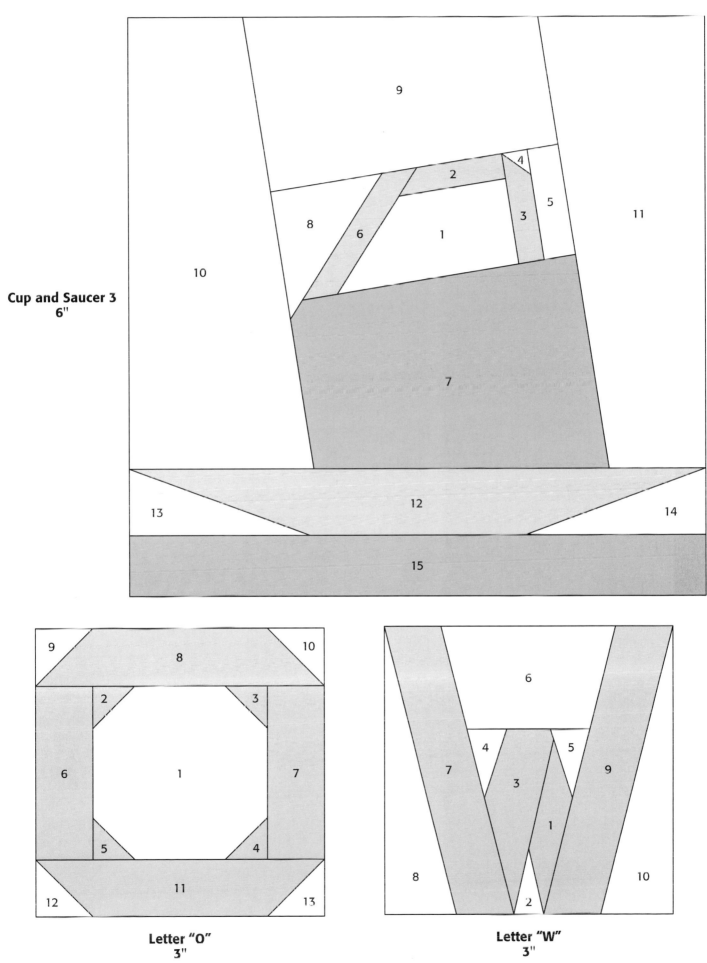

Cup and Saucer 3
6"

Letter "O"
3"

Letter "W"
3"

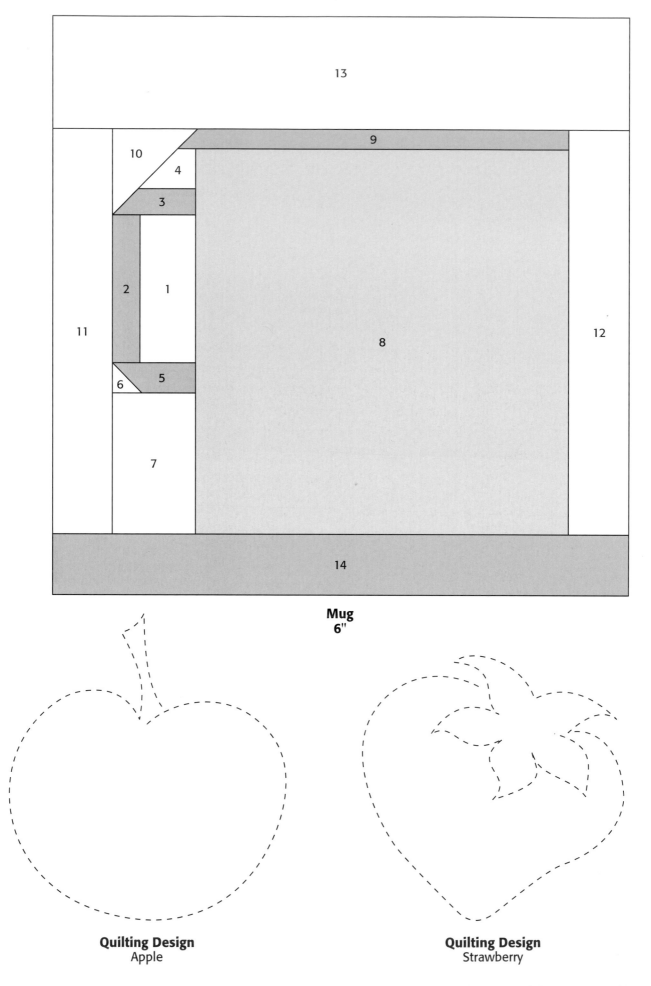

Mug
6"

Quilting Design
Apple

Quilting Design
Strawberry

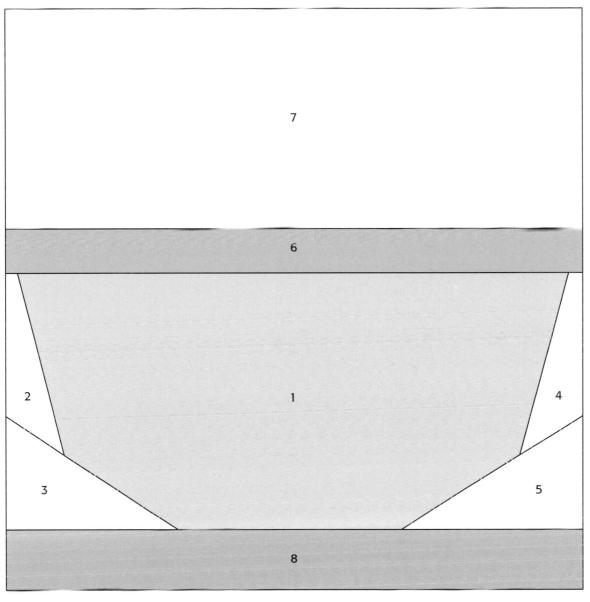

Bowl
6"

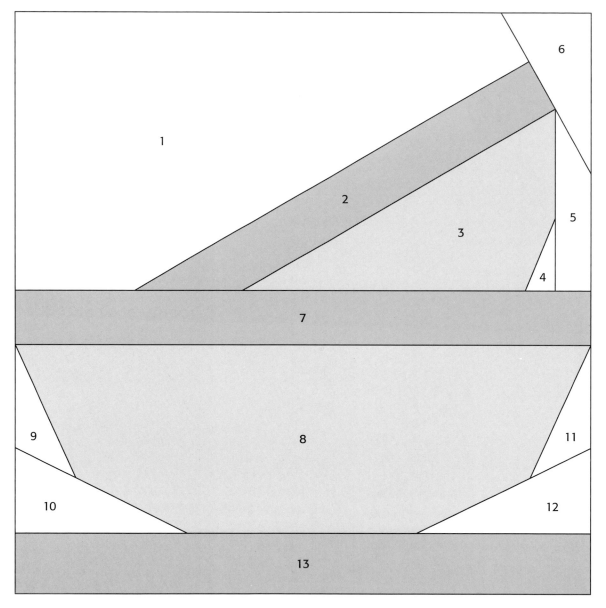

Two Bowls
6"

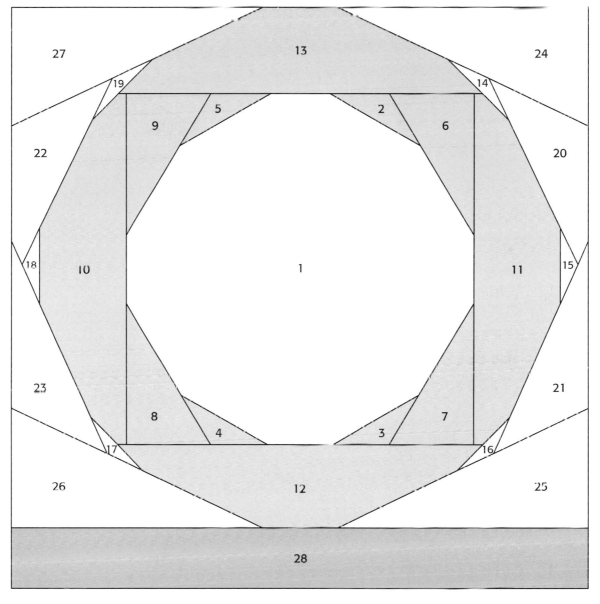

Plate
6"

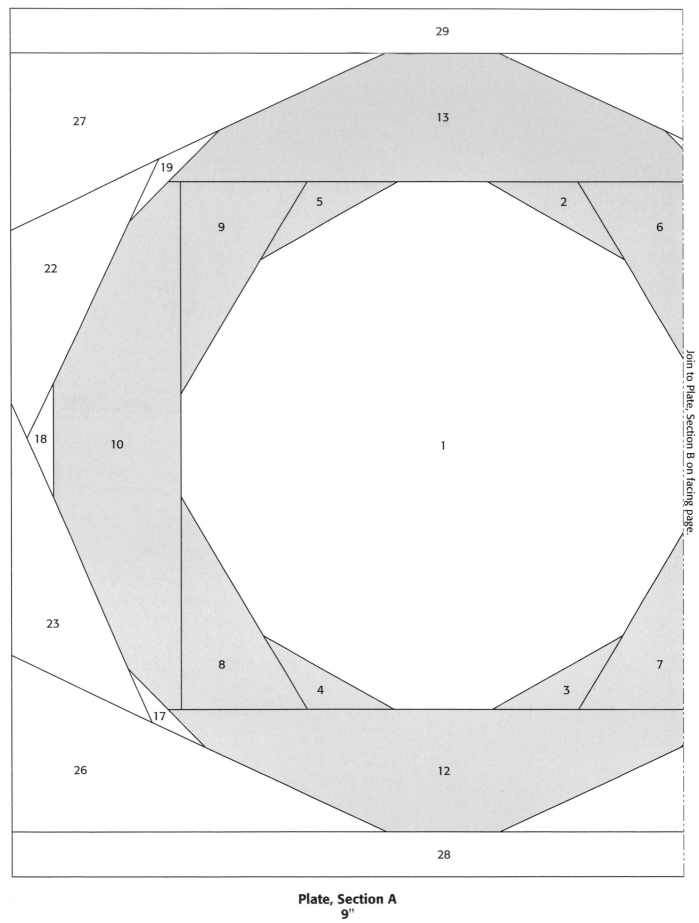

Join to Plate, Section B on facing page.

Plate, Section A
9"

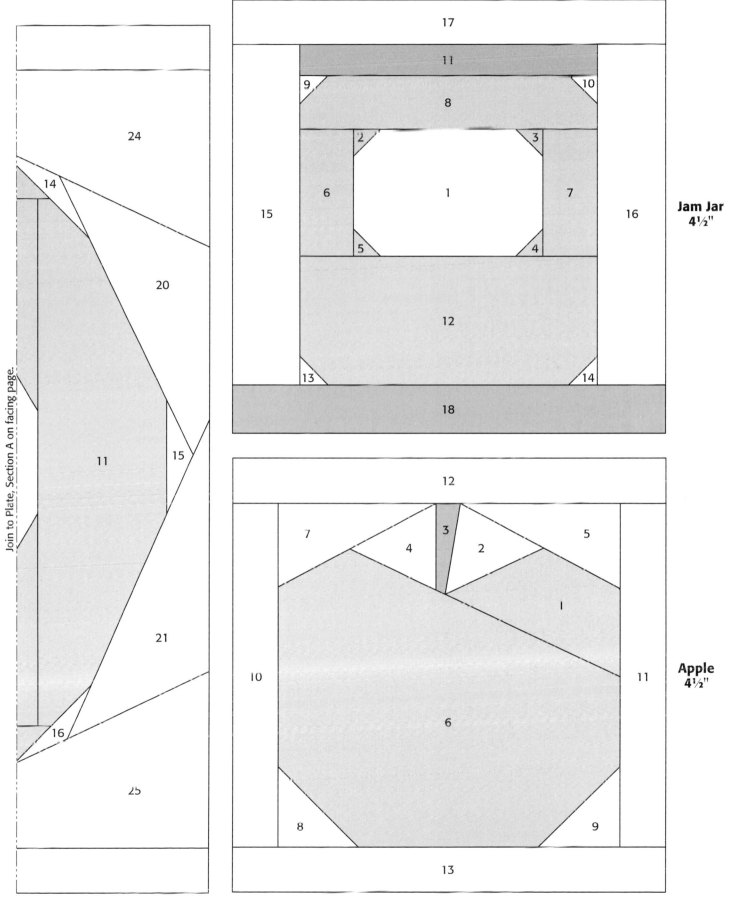

**Jam Jar
4½"**

**Apple
4½"**

**Plate, Section B
9"**

Join to Plate, Section A on facing page.

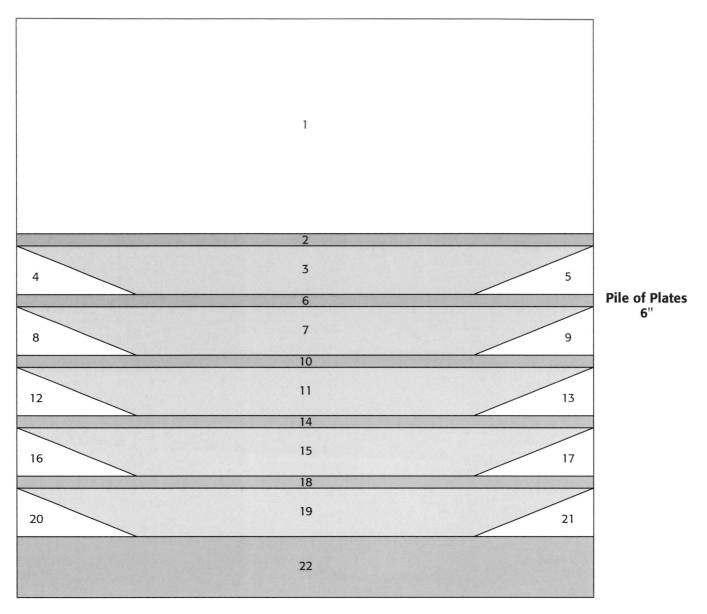

Pile of Plates
6"

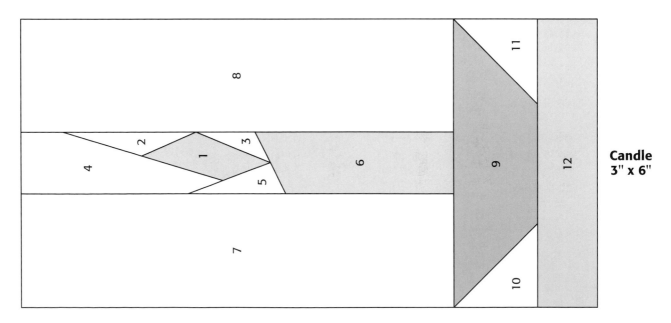

Candle
3" x 6"

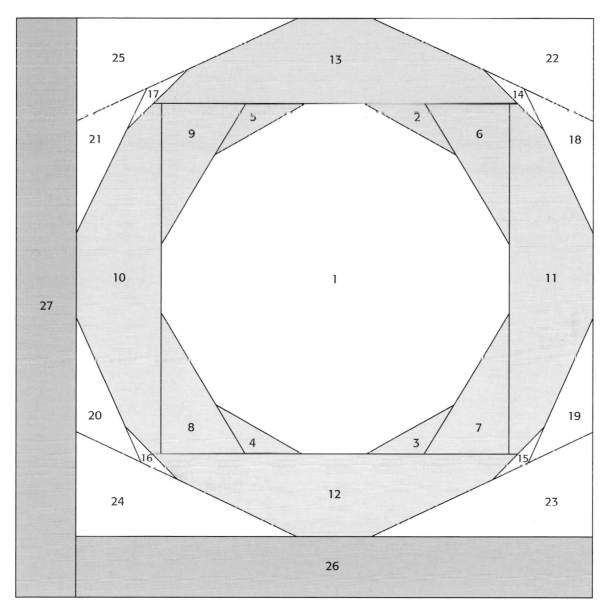

Plate in Corner
6"

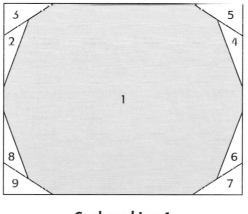

Cupboard Leg 1
2" x 2½"

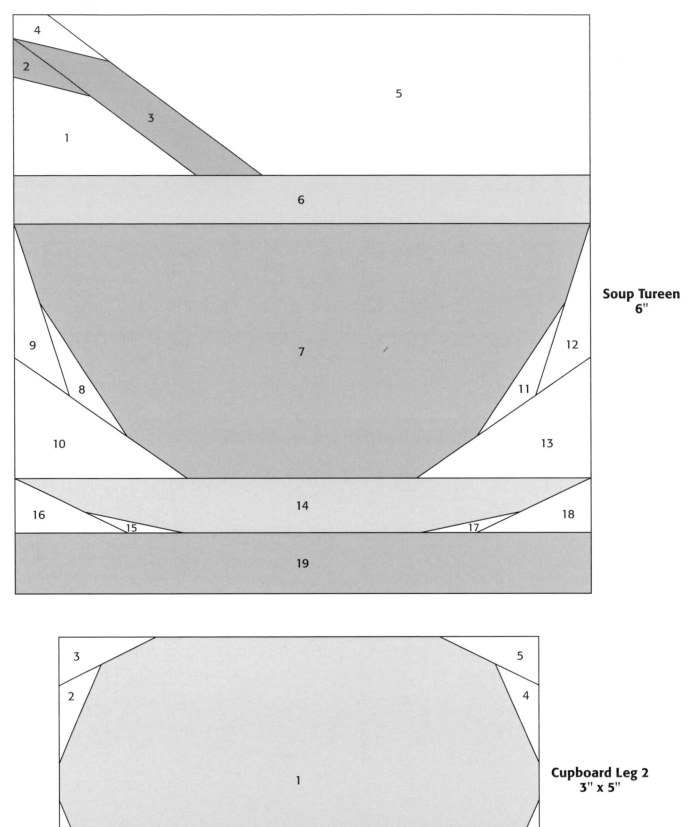

Soup Tureen
6"

Cupboard Leg 2
3" x 5"

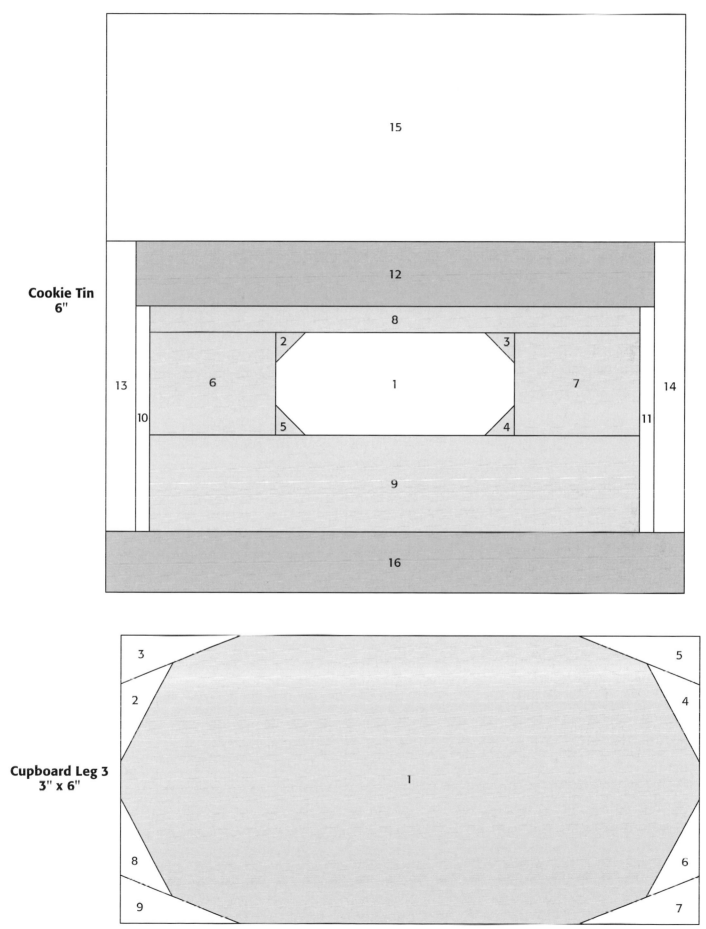

Cookie Tin
6"

Cupboard Leg 3
3" x 6"

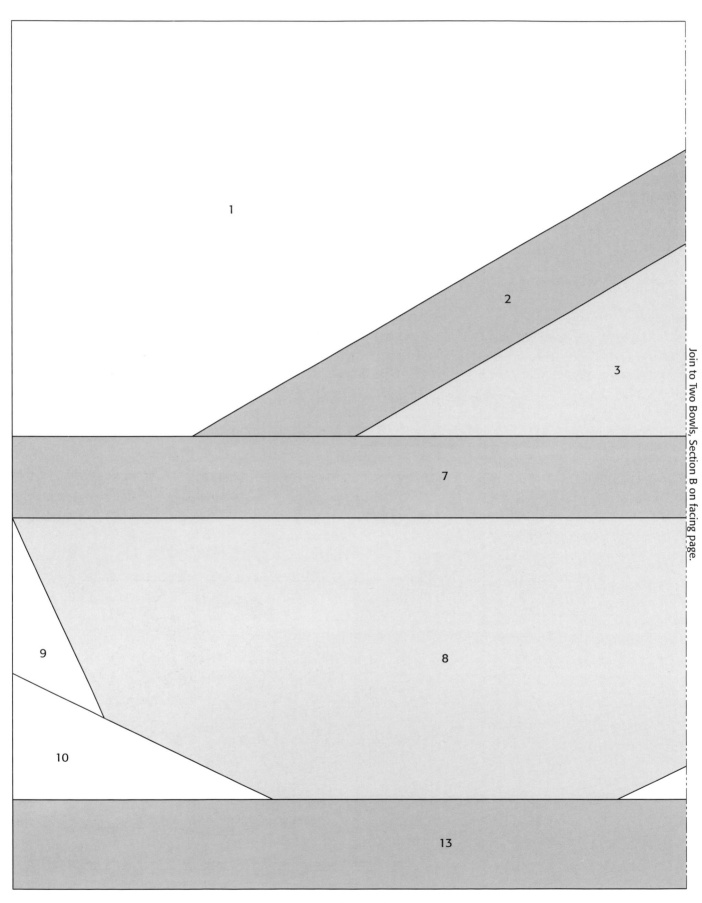

Two Bowls, Section A
9"

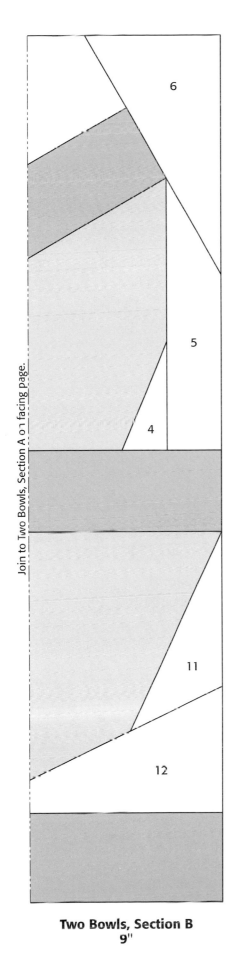

Join to Two Bowls, Section A o˥ facing page.

Two Bowls, Section B
9"

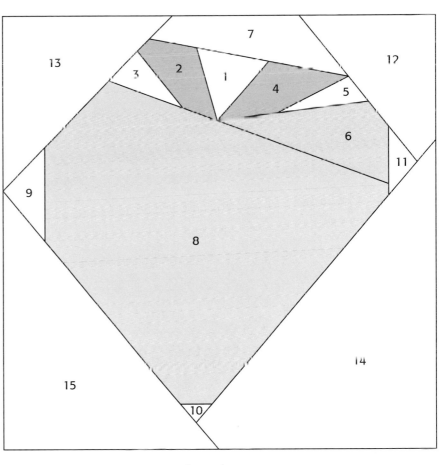

Strawberry
4½"

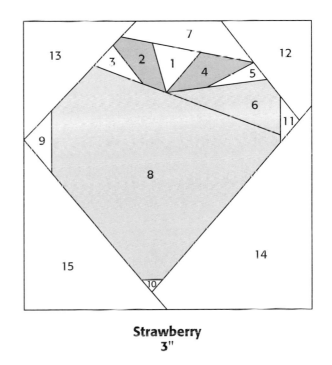

Strawberry
3"

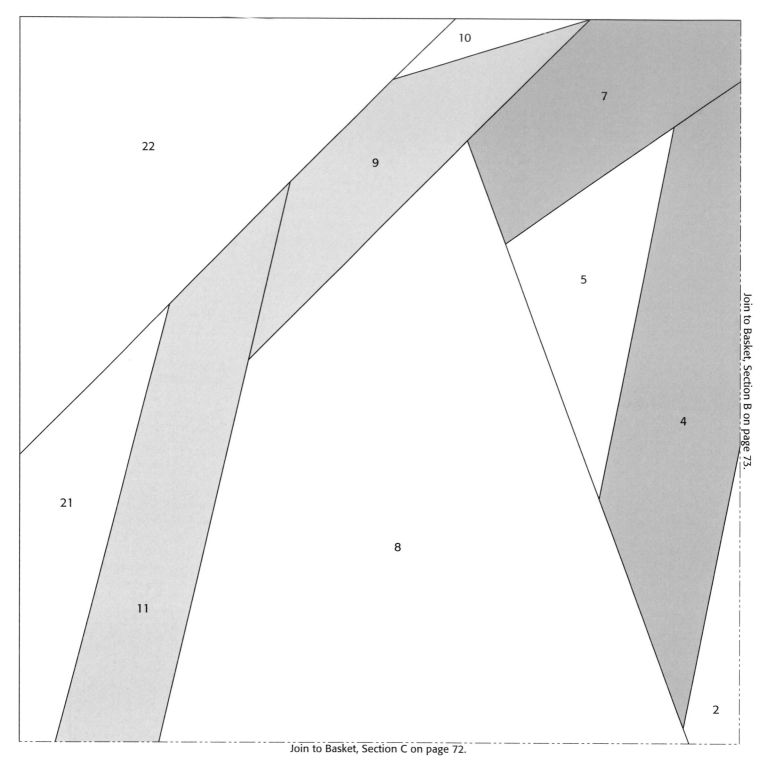

Join to Basket, Section B on page 73.

Join to Basket, Section C on page 72.

Basket, Section A
15"

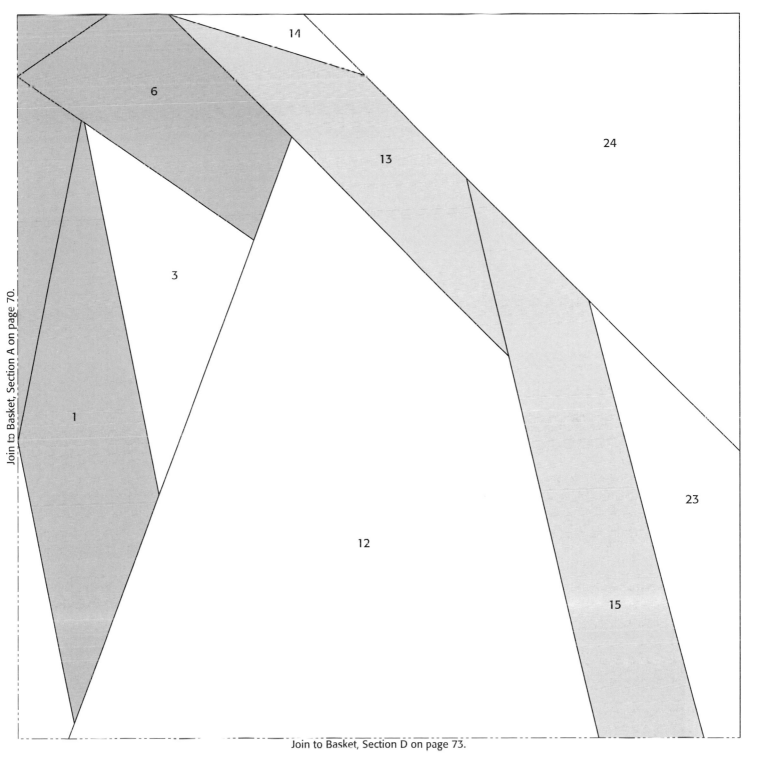

Basket, Section B
15"

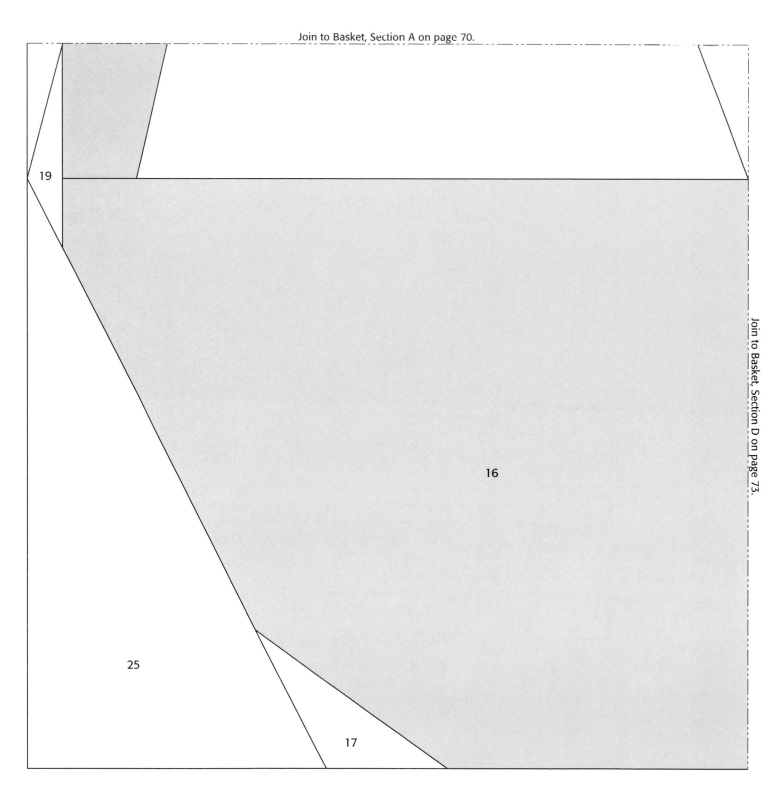

Join to Basket, Section A on page 70.

Join to Basket, Section D on page 73.

19

16

25

17

Basket, Section C
15"

Join to Basket, Section B on page 71.

Join to Basket, Section C on page 72.

20

26

18

Basket, Section D
15"

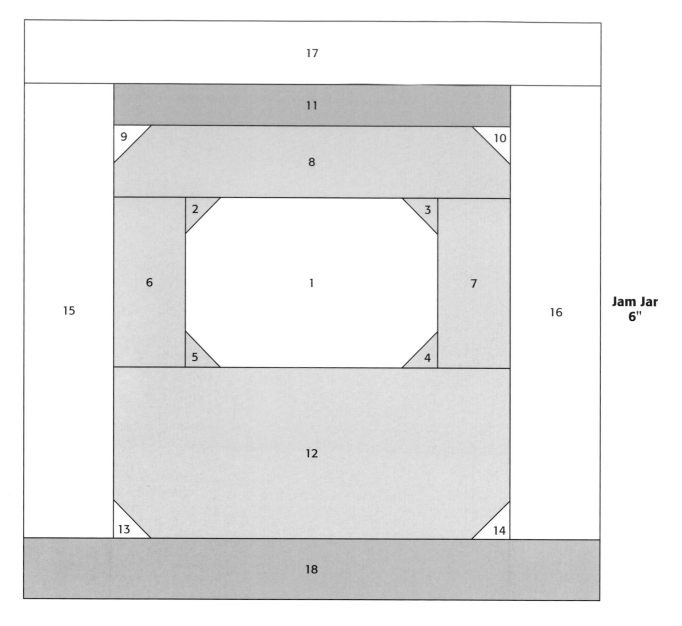

**Jam Jar
6"**

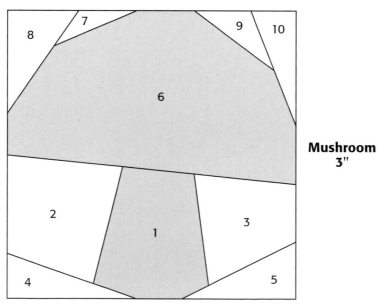

**Mushroom
3"**

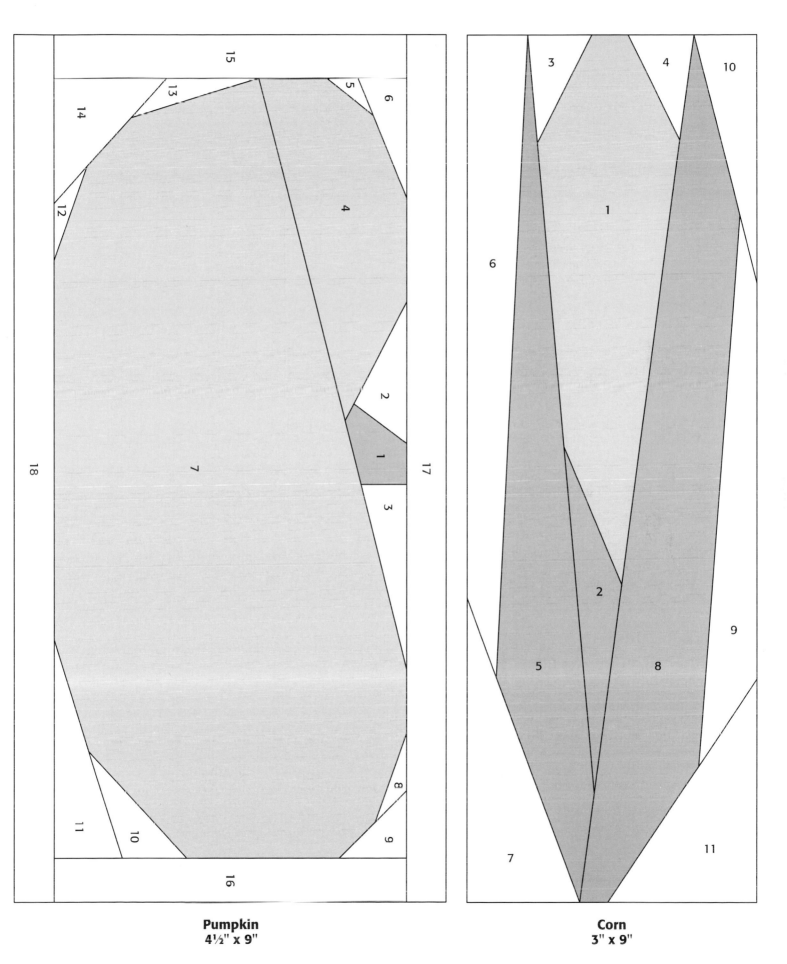

Pumpkin
4½" x 9"

Corn
3" x 9"

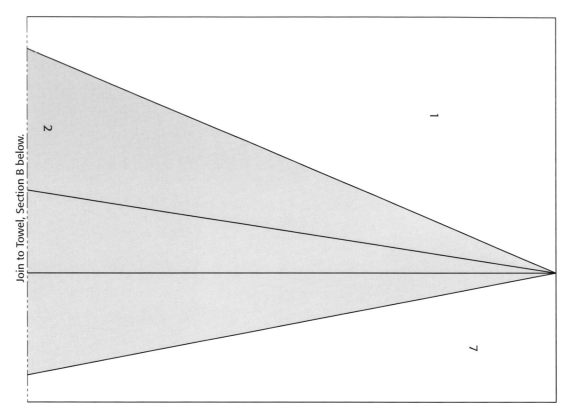

Towel, Section A
4" x 11"

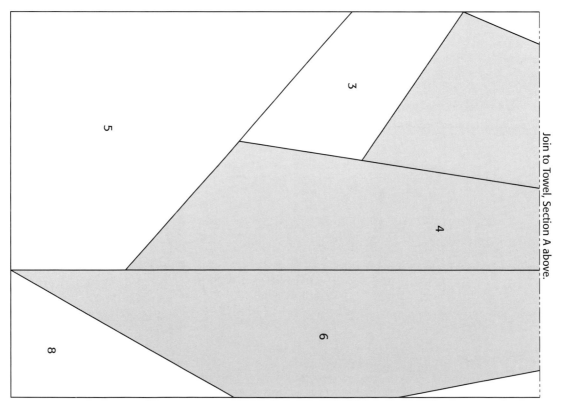

Towel, Section B
4" x 11"

Quilting Design
Flower for "Harvest"

Quilting Design
Flower for "Autumn Place Mats"
and "Delft Ceramics"

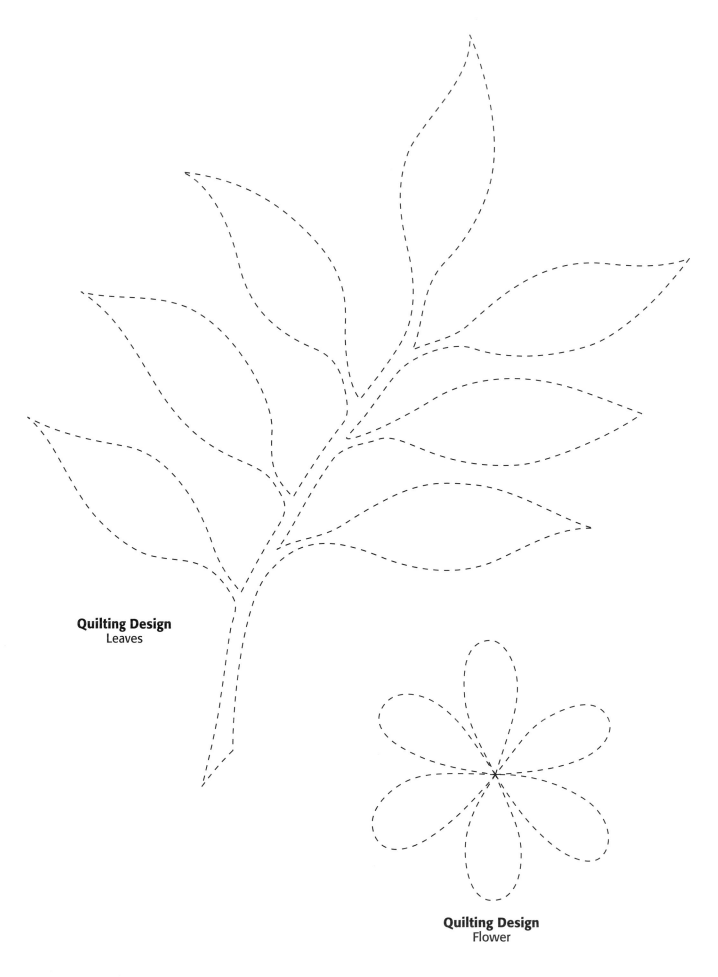

Quilting Design
Leaves

Quilting Design
Flower

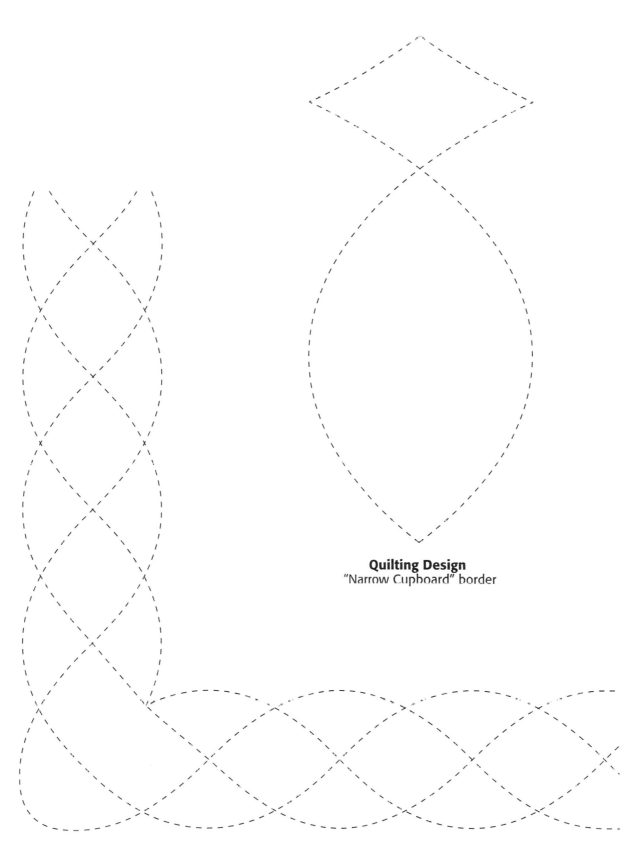

Quilting Design
"Narrow Cupboard" border

Quilting Design
"Breakfast" border

ABOUT THE AUTHOR

Maaike Bakker was born in 1958 in the Netherlands. As a child she was always busy with textile techniques (sewing, weaving, spinning). Later she studied textile techniques and art history at a teacher training college and at an art academy. In 1978 she created her first quilt as a wedding present for her friends. After a visit to Virginia and North Carolina in 1993, Maaike became very enthusiastic about paper piecing and foundation piecing. In 1997 she published her first book, *Paper Piecing,* in the Netherlands. Two years later she published her second book about this technique.

Maaike lives and works in Diever, a little village in the north of the Netherlands. Diever is famous for its open-air plays by Shakespeare, which have been held there every year since 1946. (Maaike made the costumes for these plays for thirteen years.) Maaike's studio/shop is located in an old farmhouse. Here she designs her quilts and sells quilts, fabrics, and quilting tools. She also teaches patchwork and quilting. Her studio is the basis for the quilt group As You Quilt It. The members of this group helped her make the quilts for this book.

Maaike and her husband, Theo, have three children—two daughters, ages 18 and 9, and one son, who is 15. Their oldest daughter has made a quilt every year since she was 12; their son made a quilt when he was 11. The youngest daughter is now making her first quilt.